JEWISH PORTRAITS.

" *The pedlar and hawker fathers, with their packs cast off, were priests and teachers too.*"

JEWISH PORTRAITS

BY

LADY KATIE MAGNUS

Essay Index Reprint Series

BOOKS FOR LIBRARIES PRESS
FREEPORT, NEW YORK

First Published 1888
Reprinted 1972

Library of Congress Cataloging in Publication Data

Magnus, Katie (Emanuel) Lady, 1844-1924.
    Jewish portraits.

    (Essay index reprint series)
    Reprint of the 1888 ed.
    CONTENTS: Jehudah Halevi.--The story of a street.--
Heinrich Heine. [etc.]
    1. Jews--Biography. 2. Jews--Charities.
I. Title.
DS115.M18 1972   920'.0092'924   72-3396
ISBN 0-8369-2912-8

PRINTED IN THE UNITED STATES OF AMERICA

"THESE, TO HIS MEMORY."

FEBRUARY 7 : JANUARY 11.

PREFACE.

—◆—

THE papers which form this volume
have already appeared in the pages of
Good Words, *Macmillan's Magazine*,
The National Review, and *The Spec-
tator*, and are reprinted with the very
kindly given permission of the editors.
The Frontispiece is reproduced through
the kindness of the proprietors of *Good
Words*.

I fancy that there is enough of family
likeness, and I hope there is enough of
friendly interest, in these Jewish portraits to justify their re-appearance in a
little gallery to themselves.

KATIE MAGNUS.

CONTENTS.

Jewish Portraits.

—◦—

JEHUDAH HALEVI.

PHYSICIAN AND POET.

In the far-off days, when religion was
not a habit, but an emotion, there lived
a little-known poet who solved the
pathetic puzzle of how to sing the
Lord's song in a strange land. Minor
poets of the period in plenty had essayed
a like task, leaving a literature the very
headings of which are strange to unin-
structed ears. "*Piyutim*," "*Selichoth*,"
what meaning do these words convey to

most of us? And yet they stand for
songs of exile, sung by patient generations of men who tell a monotonous tale
of mournful times—

> " When ancient griefs
> Are closely veiled
> In recent shrouds,"

as one of the anonymous host expresses
it. For the writers were of the race of
the traditional Sweet Singer, and their
lot was cast in those picturesquely dis-
appointing Middle Ages, too close to
the chivalry of the time to appreciate
its charm. One pictures these comparatively cultured pariahs, these gaber-
dined, degenerate descendants of seers
and prophets, looking out from their
ghettoes on a world which, for all the
stir and bustle of barbaric life, was to
them as desolate and as bare of promise
of safe resting-place as when the waters
covered it, and only the tops of the
mountains appeared. One sees them

now as victims, and now as spectators
but never as actors in that strange show,
yet always, we fancy, realizing the
barbarism, and with that undoubting
faith of theirs in the ultimate dawning
of a perfect day, seeming to regard the
long reign of brute force, of priestcraft,
and of ignorance as phases of misrule,
which, like unto manifold others, should
pass whilst they would endure.

> " A race that has been tested
> And tried through fire and water,
> Is surely prized by Thee,"

cries out a typical bard, with, perhaps, a
too-conscious tone of martyrdom, and a
decided tendency to clutch at the halo.
The attitude is altogether a trifle arro-
gant and stolid and defiant to superficial
criticism, but one for which a deeper
insight will find excuses. The com-
placency is not quite self-complacency,
the pride is impersonal, and so though
provoking, is pathetic too. Something

of the old longing which, with a sort of
satisfied negation, claimed "honour and
glory," "not unto us," but unto "the
Name," seems to find expression again
in the unrhymed and often unrhythmical
compositions of these patient poets of
the *Selicha.* Their poetry, perhaps,
goes some way towards explaining their
patience, for, undoubtedly, there is no
doggedness like that of men who at will,
and by virtue of their own thoughts,
can soar above circumstances and surroundings. "Vulgar minds," says a
last-century poet, truly enough, "refuse
or crouch beneath their load," and inevitably such will collapse under a
pressure which the cultivated will endure, and "bear without repining."
The ills to which flesh is heir will
generally be best and most bravely
borne by those to whom the flesh is
not all in all ; as witness Heine, whose
voice rose at its sweetest, year after

year, from his mattress grave. That
there never was a time in all their
history when the lusts of the flesh were
a whole and satisfying ambition to the
Jew, or when the needs of the body
bounded his desires, may account in
some degree for that marvellous capacity
for suffering which the race has evinced.

These rugged *Piyutim*, for over a
thousand years, come in from most
parts of the continent of Europe as a
running commentary on its laws, suggest-
ing a new reading for the old significant
connection between a country's lays and
its legislation, and supplying an illustration, to Charles Kingsley's dictum, that
"the literature of a nation is its auto-
biography." *Selicha* (from the Hebrew,
סלחה) means literally forgiveness, and to
forgive and to be forgiven is the burden
and the refrain of most of the so-called
Penitential Poems (*Selichoth*), whose
theme is of sorrows and persecutions

past telling, almost past praying about.
Piyut (derived from the Greek ποιητής)
in early Jewish writings stood for the
poet himself, and later on it was applied
as a generic name for his compositions.
From the second to the eighth century
there is decidedly more suggestion of
martyrdom than of minstrelsy in these
often unsigned and always unsingable
sonnets of the synagogue, and especially
about the contributions from France, and
subsequently from Germany, to the
liturgical literature of the Middle Ages,
there is a far too prevailing note of the
swan's song for cheerful reading. Hap-
pier in their circumstances than the rest
of their European co-religionists, the
Spanish writers sing, for the most part,
in clearer and higher strains, and it is
they who, towards the close of the tenth
century, first add something of the grace
and charm of metrical versification to
the hitherto crude and rough style of

composition which had sufficed. Even about the prose of these Spanish authors there is many a light and happy touch, and, not unseldom, in the voluminous and somewhat verbose literature, we come across a short story (*midrash*) or a pithy saying, with salt enough of wit or of pathos about it to make its preservation through the ages quite comprehensible.

Hep, Hep, was the dominant note in the European concert, when at the beginning of the twelfth century our poet was born. France, Italy, Germany, Bohemia, and Greece had each been, at different times within the hundred years which had just closed, the scene of terrible persecutions. In Spain alone, under the mild sway of the Omneyade Kaliphs, there had been a tolerably long entr'acte in the "fifteen hundred year tragedy" that the Jewish race was enacting, and there, in old

Castille, whilst Alfonso VI. was king,
Jehudah Halevi passed his childhood.
Although in 1085 Alfonso was already
presiding over an important confedera-
tion of Catholic States, yet at the
beginning of the twelfth century the
Arab supremacy in Spain was still comparatively unshaken, and its influence,
social and political, over its Jewish
subjects was still paramount. Perhaps
the one direction in which that impressionable race was least perceptibly
affected by its Arab experiences was in
its literature. And remembering how
distinctly in the elder days of art the
influence of Greek thought is traceable
in Jewish philosophy, it is very strange
to note with these authors of the Middle
Ages, who write as readily in Arabic as
in Hebrew, that, though the hand is the
hand of Esau, the voice remains unmis-
takeably the voice of Jacob. Munk
dwells on this remarkable distinction in

the poetry of the period, and, with some natural preference perhaps, strives to account for it in the wide divergence of the Hebrew and Arabic sources of inspiration. The poetry of the Jews he roundly declares to be universal, and that of the Arabs egotistic in its tendency ; the sons of the desert finding subjects for their Muse in traditions of national glory and in dreams of material delight, whilst the descendants of prophets turn to the records of their own ancestry, and find their themes in remorseful memories, and in unselfish and unsensual hopes. With the Jewish poet, past and future are alike uncoloured by personal desire, and even the sins and sufferings of his race he enshrines in song. If it be good, as a modern writer has declared it to be, that a nation should commemorate its defeats, certainly no race has ever been richer in such subjects, or has shown itself more willing, in ritual and rhyme, to take advantage of them.

Whilst the leaders of society, the licentious crusader and the celibate monk, were stumbling so sorely in the shadow of the Cross, and whilst the rank and file throughout Europe were steeped in deepest gloom of densest ignorance and superstition, the lamp of learning, handed down from generation to generation of despised Jews, was still being carefully trimmed, and was burning at its brightest among the little knot of philosophers and poets in Spain. Alcharisi, the commentator and critic of the circle, gives, for his age, a curiously high standard of the qualifications essential to the sometimes lightly bestowed title of authorship. "A poet," he says, "(1) must be perfect in metre; (2) his language of classic purity; (3) the subject of his poem worthy of the poet's best skill, and calculated to instruct and to elevate mankind; (4) his style

must be full of 'lucidity' and free from
every obscure or foreign expression ; (5)
he must never sacrifice sense to sound ;
(6) he must add infinite care and patience
to his gift of genius, never submitting
crude work to the world ; and (7) lastly,
he must neither parade all he knows nor
offer the winnowings of his harvest."

These seem sufficiently severe conditions even to nineteenth-century judgment, but Jehudah Halevi, say his
admirers and even his contemporaries,
fulfilled them all.

That a man should be judged by his
peers gives a promise of sound and honest testimony, and if such judgment be
accepted as final then does Halevi hold
high rank indeed among men and poets.
One of the first things that strike an
intruder into this old-world literary circle
is the curious absence of those small
rivalries and jealousies which we of other
times and manners look instinctively to

find.   Such records as remain to us make certainly less amusing reading than some later biographies and autobiographies afford, but, on the other hand, it has an unique interest of its own, to come upon authentic traces of such susceptible beings as authors, all living in the same set and with a limited range both of subjects and of readers, who yet live together in harmony, and interchange sonnets and epigrams curiously free from every suggestion of envy, hatred, or uncharitableness.   There is, in truth, a wonderful freshness of sentiment about these gentle old scholars.   They say pretty things to and of each other in almost school-girl fashion.   " I pitch my tent in thy heart," exclaims one as he sets out on a journey. More poetically Halevi expresses a similar sentiment to a friend of his (Ibn Giat) :

> " If to the clouds thy boldness wings its flight,
>   Within our hearts, thou ne'er art out of sight."

Writes another (Moses Aben Ezra), and he was a philosopher and grammarian to boot, one not to be lightly suspected of sentimentality, "Our hearts were as one : now parted from thee, my heart is divided into two." Halevi was the absent friend in this instance, and he begins his response as warmly :—

> " How can I rest when we are absent one from
> another?
> Were it not for the glad hope of thy return
> The day which tore thee from me
> Would tear me from all the world."

Or the note changes : some disappointment or disillusion is hinted at, and under its influence our tender-hearted poet complains to this same sympathetic correspondent, " I was asked, Hast thou sown the seed of friendship ? My answer was, Alas, I did, but the seed did not thrive."

It is altogether the strangest, soberest little picture of sweetness and light, showing beneath the gaudy, tawdry phantas-

magoria of the age.   Rub away the paint
and varnish from the hurrying host of
crusaders, from the confused crowd of
dreary, deluded rabble, and there they
stand like a " restored" group, these tune-
ful, unworldly sages, "toiling, rejoicing,
sorrowing," with Jehudah Halevi, poet
and physician, as central figure.   For,
loyal to the impulse which in times long
past had turned Akiba into a herdsman
and had induced Hillel in his youth and
poverty to " hire himself out wherever he
could find a job,"[1] which, in the time to
come, was to make of Maimonides a
diamond cutter, and of Spinoza an opti-
cian, Halevi compounded simples as
conscientiously as he composed sonnets,
and was more of doctor than of poet by
profession.   He was true to those traditions and instincts of his race, which,
through all the ages, had recognized the
dignity of labour and had inclined to use

[1] Talmud, Yoma 356.

literature as a staff rather than as a crutch. His prescriptions were probably such as the Pharmacopœia of to-day might hardly approve, and the spirit in which he prescribed, one must own, is perhaps also a little out of date. Here is a grace just before physic which brings to one's mind the advice given by a famous divine of the muscular Christianity school to his young friend at Oxford, "Work hard— as for your degree, leave it to God."

> " God grant that I may rise again,
> Nor perish by Thine anger slain.
> This draught that I myself combine,
> What is it ? Only Thou dost know
> If well or ill, if swift or slow,
> Its parts shall work upon my pain.
> Ay of these things, alone is Thine
> The knowledge. All my faith I place,
> Not in my craft, but in Thy grace." [1] (1)

Halevi's character, however, was far enough removed from that which an old author has defined as "pious and paine-

[1] The extracts marked thus (1) have been done into verse from the German of Geiger, by Miss Amy Levy.

full." He "entered the courts with gladness:" his religion being of a healthy, happy, natural sort, free from all affectations, and with no taint either of worldliness or of other worldliness to be discerned in it. Perhaps our poet was not entirely without that comfortable consciousness of his own powers and capabilities which, in weaker natures, turns its seamy side to us as conceit, nor altogether free from that impatience of "fools" which seems to be another of the temptations of the gifted. This rather ill-tempered little extract which we are honest enough to append appears to indicate as much :—

> "Lo ! my light has pierced to the dark abyss,
>   I have brought forth gems from the gloomy mine ;
> Now the fools would see them ! I ask you this :
>   Shall I fling my pearls down before the swine ?
> From the gathered cloud shall the raindrops flow
> To the barren land where no fruit can grow ?" (1)

The little grumble is characteristic, but in actual fact no land was "barren" to

his hopeful sunny temperament. In the
" morning he sowed his seed, and in the
evening he withheld not his hand," and
from his " gathered clouds," the raindrops
fell rainbow-tinted. The love songs,
which a trustworthy tradition tells us were
written to his wife, are quite as beautiful
in their very different way as an impassioned elegy he wrote when death claimed
his friend, Aben Ezra, or as the famous
ode he composed on Jerusalem. Halevi
wrote prose too, and a bulky volume in
Arabic is in existence, which sets forth
the history of a certain Bulan, king of
the Khozars, who reigned, the antiqua-
rians agree, about the beginning of the
eighth century, over a territory situate
on the shores of the Caspian Sea. This
Bulan would seem to have been of a
hesitating, if not of a sceptical, turn of
mind in religious matters. Honestly
anxious to be correct in his opinions, his
anxiety becomes intensified by means of

a vision, and he finally summons representative followers of Moses, of Jesus, and of Mahomet to discuss in his presence the tenets of their masters. These chosen doctors of divinity argue at great length, and the Jewish Rabbi is said to have best succeeded in satisfying the anxious scruples of the king. The same authorities tell us that Bulan became an earnest convert to Judaism, and commenced in his own person a Jewish dynasty which endured for more than two centuries. Over these more or less historic facts Halevi casts the glamour of his genius, and makes, at any rate, a very readable story out of them, which incidentally throws some valuable side lights on his own way of regarding things. Unluckily, side lights are all we possess, in place of the electric illuminating fashion of the day. Those copious details, which our grandchildren seem likely to inherit concerning all and sundry of

this generation, are wholly wanting to us,
the earlier heirs of time. Of Halevi, as
of greater poets, who have lived even
nearer to our own age, history speaks
neither loudly nor in chorus. Yet, for
our consolation, there is the reflection
that the various and varying records of
" Thomas's ideal John : never the real
John, nor John's John, but often very,
unlike either," may, in truth, help us but
little to a right comprehension of the
" real John, known only to His Maker."
Once get at a man's ideals, it has been
well said, and the rest is easy. And thus
though our facts are but few and frag-
mentary concerning the man of whom
one admirer quaintly says that, " created
in the image of God" could in his case
stand for literal description, yet may we,
by means of his ideals, arrive perhaps at
a juster conception of Halevi's charming
personality than did we possess the very
pen with which he wrote and the desk

at which he sat and the minutest and most authentic particulars as to his wont of using both.

His ideal of religion was expressed in every practical detail of daily life.

> " When I remove from Thee, O God,
> I die whilst I live ; but when
> I cleave to Thee, I live in death." [1]

These three lines indicate the sentiment of Judaism, and might almost serve as sufficient sample of Halevi's simple creed, for, truth to tell, the religion of the Jews does not concern itself greatly with the ideal, being of a practical rather than of an emotional sort, rigid as to practice, but tolerant over theories, and inquiring less as to a man's belief than as to his conduct. Work—steady, cheerful, untiring work—was perhaps Halevi's favourite form of praise. Still, being a poet he sings, and, like the birds, in divers strains, with happy, unconscious

[1] From Atonement Service.

effort. Only " For Thy songs, O
God!" he cries, "my heart is a harp;"
and truly enough, in some of these
ancient Hebrew hymns, the stately intensity of which it is impossible to re-
produce, we seem to hear clearly the
human strings vibrate. The truest faith,
the most living hope, the widest charity,
is breathed forth in them ; and they
have naturally been enshrined by his
fellow-believers in the most sacred parts
of their liturgy, quotations from which
would here obviously be out of place.
Some dozen lines only shall be given,
and these chosen in illustration of the
universality of the Jewish hope. " Where
can I find Thee, O God ? " the poet
questions ; and there is wonderfully little
suggestion of reserved places about the
answer :—

> " Lord ! where art Thou to be found ?
> Hidden and high is Thy home.
> And where shall we find Thee not ?
> Thy glory fills the world.

Thou art found in my heart,
And at the uttermost ends of the earth.
A refuge for the near,
For the far, a trust.

" The universe cannot contain Thee ;
How then a temple's shrine ?
Though Thou art raised above men
On Thy high and lofty throne,
Yet art Thou near unto them
In their spirit and in their flesh.
Who can say he has not seen Thee ?
When lo ! the heavens and their host
Tell of Thy fear, in silent testimony.

" I sought to draw near to Thee.
With my whole heart I sought Thee,
And when I went out to meet Thee,
To meet me, Thou wast ready on the road.
In the wonders of Thy might
And in Thy holiness I have beheld Thee.
Who is there that should not fear Thee ?
The yoke of Thy kingdom is for ever and for all,
Who is there that should not call upon Thee ?
Thou givest unto all their food."

Concerning Halevi's ideal of love and
marriage we may speak at greater
length ; and on these subjects one may
remark that our poet's ideal was less
individual than national. Mixing inti-
mately among men who, as a matter of

course, bestowed their fickle favours on
several wives, and whose poetic notion of
matrimony—on the prosaic we will not
touch—was a houri-peopled Paradise, it
is perhaps to the credit of the Jews that
this was one of the Arabian customs
which, with all their susceptibility, they
were very slow to adopt. Halevi, as is
the general faithful fashion of his race,
all his life long loved one only, and clave
to her—a "dove of rarest worth, and
sweet. exceedingly," as in one of his
poems he declares her to be. The test
of poetry, Goethe somewhere says, is the
substance which remains when the poetry
is reduced to prose. When the poetry
has been yet further reduced by succes-
sive processes of translation, the test
becomes severe. We fancy, though,
that there is still some considerable resi-
duum about Halevi's songs to his old-
fashioned love—his Ophrah, as he calls
her in some of them. Here is one when

they are likely to be parted for a
while :—

" So we must be divided ; sweetest, stay,
　　Once more, mine eyes would seek thy glance's
　　　light.
　At night I shall recall thee : Thou, I pray,
　　Be mindful of the days of our delight.
　Come to me in my dreams, I ask of thee,
　And even in my dreams be gentle unto me.

" If thou shouldst send me greeting in the grave,
　　The cold breath of the grave itself were sweet ;
　Oh, take my life, my life, 'tis all I have,
　　If it should make thee live, I do entreat.
　I think that I shall hear when I am dead,
　The rustle of thy gown, thy footsteps overhead." (1)

And another, which reads like a marriage hymn :—

　　　" A dove of rarest worth
　　　　And sweet exceedingly ;
　　　Alas, why does she turn
　　　　And fly so far from me ?
　　　In my fond heart a tent,
　　　　Should aye preparèd be.
　　　My poor heart she has caught
　　　With magic spells and wiles.
　　　I do not sigh for gold,
　　　But for her mouth that smiles ;
　　　Her hue it is so bright,
　　　She half makes blind my sight,
　　　　*　　　*　　　*　　　*

> The day at last is here
> Filled full of love's sweet fire ;
> The twain shall soon be one,
> Shall stay their fond desire.
> Ah ! would my tribe could chance
> On such deliverance." (1)

On a first reading, these last two lines strike one as oddly out of place in a love poem. But as we look again, they seem to suggest, that in a nature so full and wholesome as Halevi's, love did not lead to a selfish forgetfulness, nor marriage mean a joy which could hold by its side no care for others. Rather to prove that love at its best does not narrow the sympathies, but makes them widen and broaden out to enfold the less fortunate under its happy, brooding wings. And though at the crowning moment of his life Halevi could spare a tender thought for his "tribe," with very little right could the foolish, favourite epithet of "tribalism" be flung at him, and with even less of justice at his race. In truth, they were

3

" patriots " in the sorriest, sincerest sense
—this dispossessed people, who owned
not an inch of the lands wherein they
wandered, from the east unto the west.
It is prejudice or ignorance maybe, but
certainly it is not history, which sees the
Jews as any but the faithfullest of citizens to their adopted States ; faithful,
indeed, often to the extent of forgetting,
save in set and prayerful phrases, the
lost land of their fathers. Here is a
typical national song of the twelfth century, in which no faintest echo of regret
or of longing for other glories, other
shrines, can be discerned :—

> " I found that words could ne'er express
>   The half of all its loveliness ;
> From place to place I wandered wide,
> With amorous sight unsatisfied,
> Till last I reached all cities' queen,
>   Tolaitola [1] the fairest seen.
>
>   *   *   *   *
>
> Her palaces that show so bright
> In splendour, shamed the starry height,

---

[1] Hebrew for Toledo.

> Whilst temples in their glorious sheen
> Rivalled the glories that had been ;
> With earnest reverent spirit there,
> The pious soul breathes forth its prayer."

The " earnest reverent spirit" may be a little out of drawing now, but that "fairest city seen" of the Spanish poet,[1] might well stand for the London or Paris of to-day in the well-satisfied, cosmopolitan affections of an ordinary Englishman or Frenchman of the Jewish faith. And which of us may blame this adaptability, this comfortable inconstancy of content? Widows and widowers remarry, and childless folks, it is said, grow quite foolishly fond of adopted kin. With practical people the past is past, and to the prosperous nothing comes more easy than forgetting. After all—

> " What can you do with people when they are dead?
> But if you are pious, sing a hymn and go ;
> Or, if you are tender, heave a sigh and go.
> But go by all means, and permit the grass
> To keep its green fend 'twixt them and you,"[2]

---

[1] Alcharisi.   [2] E. B. Browning.

In the long centuries since Jerusalem
fell there has been time and to spare for
the green grass to wither into dusty
weeds above those desolate dead whose
"place knows them no more." That
Halevi with his "poetic heart," which is
a something different from the most
metrical of poetic imaginations, cherished
a closer ideal of patriotism than some
of his brethren may not be denied.
"Israel among the nations," he writes,
"is as the heart among the limbs." He
was the loyalest of Spanish subjects, yet
Jerusalem was to him, in sober fact, "the
city of the world."

In these learned latter days, the tiniest
crumbs of tradition have been so eagerly
pounced upon by historians to analyze
and argue over, that we are almost left
in doubt whether the very A B C of our
own history may still be writ in old
English characters. The process which
has bereft the bogy uncle of our youthful

belief of his hump, and all but transformed the Bluebeard of the British
throne into a model monarch, has not
spared to set its puzzling impress on the
few details which have come down to us
concerning Halevi. Whether the love
poems, some eight hundred in number,
were all written to his wife, is now questioned ; whether 1086 or 1105 is the
date of his birth, and if Toledo or Old
Castille be his birthplace, is contested.
Whether he came to a peaceful end, or
was murdered by wandering Arabs, is
left doubtful, since both the year of his
death [1] and the manner of it, are stated
in different ways by different authorities,
among whom it is hard to choose.
Whether, indeed, he ever visited the
Holy City, whether he beheld it with
"actual sight or sight of faith," is
greatly and gravely debated ; but
amidst all the bewildering dust of doubt

[1] No authority gives it later than 1140.

that the researches of wise commentators have raised, the central fact of his life is left to us undisputed. The realities they meddle with, but the ideals, happily, they leave to us undimmed. All at least agree, that " she whom the Rabbi loved was a poor woebegone darling, a moving picture of desolation, and her name was Jerusalem." There is a consensus of opinion among the critics that this often-quoted saying of Heine's was only a poetical way of putting a literal and undoubted truth. On this subject, indeed, our poet has only to speak for himself.

> " Oh ! city of the world, most chastely fair ;
>   In the far west, behold I sigh for thee.
>   And in my yearning love I do bethink me,
>   Of bygone ages ; of thy ruined fane,
>   Thy vanished splendour of a vanished day.
>   Oh ! had I eagles' wings I'd fly to thee,
>   And with my falling tears make moist thine earth.
>   I long for thee ; what though indeed thy kings
>   Have passed for ever ; though where once up-rose
>   Sweet balsam-trees the serpent makes his nest.
>   Oh ! that I might embrace thy dust, the sod
>   Were sweet as honey to my fond desire." (1)

Fifty translations cannot spoil the true ring in such fervid words as these. And in a world so sadly full of " fond desires," destined to remain for ever unfulfilled, it is pleasant to know that Halevi accomplished his. He unquestionably travelled to Palestine ; whether his steps were stayed short of Jerusalem we know not, but he undoubtedly reached the shores, and breathed " the air of that land which makes men wise," as in loving hyperbole, a more primitive patriot [1] expresses it.

And seeing how that " the Lord God doth like a printer who setteth the letters backward," [2] there is small cause, perchance, for grieving in that the breath our poet drew in the land of his dreams was the breath not of life but of death.

[1] Rabbi Seira.

[2] " The Lord God doth like a printer who setteth the letters backward ; we see and feel well His setting, but the print we shall see yonder in the life to come."— ·LUTHER'S " Table Talk."

THE STORY OF A STREET.

To the ear and eye that can find sermons in stones, streets, one would fancy,
must be brimful of suggestive stories.
There might be differences of course.
From a stone of the polished pebble
variety, for instance, one could only pre-
dict smooth platitudes, and the romance
in a block of regulation stucco would
possibly turn out a trifle prosaic. But
the right stone and the right street will
always have an eloquence of their own
for the right listener or lounger, and
certain crumbling old tenements which
were carted away as rubbish a year or
two back in Frankfort must have been

3 *

rarely gifted in this line. "Words of
fire," and "written in blood," would, in
truth, have no parabolic meaning, if the
stones of that ancient *Judengasse* suddenly took to story-telling. A long
record of sorrow, and wrong, and squalid
romance, would be unfolded, and, inasmuch as the sorrows have been healed
and the wrongs have been righted, it
may not be uninteresting to look for a
moment at the picturesque truths that
lie hidden under that squalid romance,
which, like a mist, hung for centuries
over the Jews' quarter.

The very first authentic record of
the presence of Jews in Frankfort comes
to us in the account of a massacre of
some hundred and eighty of them in
1241. This persecution was probably
epidemic rather than indigenous in its
nature, its germ distinctly traceable to
those conscientious and comprehensive
attempts of Louis the Saint, in the pre-

ceding year, to stamp out Judaism in his
dominions. At any rate, for German
Jews, an era of protection began under
Frederick Barbarossa, and the Frankfort
Jews among the rest, during the next
hundred years, enjoyed the "no history"
which to the Jewish nation, pre-eminently amongst all others, must have
been synonymous with happiness. But
the story begins again about the middle
of the fourteenth century when the Black
Plague raged, and sanitary inspection,
old style, took the form of declaring the
wells to be poisoned, and of advising the
burning and plunder of Jews by way
of antidote. Jews were prolific, their
hoards portable, their houses slightly
built, so the burnings and the massacres
and the liftings become intermittent and
a little difficult to localise, till about the
year 1430, when Frederick III., egged
on by his clergy, made an order for all
Jews in Frankfort to reside out of sight

and sound of the holy Cathedral. A
site just without the ancient walls of the
town, and belonging to the council, was
allotted to them, and here, at their own
expense, the Jews built their *Judengasse.*

The street contained originally some
hundred and ninety-six houses, and
iron-sheeted gates, kept fast closed on
Sundays and saint days, grew gradually
to be barred from inside as well as outside on the Ghetto. The pleasures and
the hopes which Jews might not share
they came by slow degrees to hate and
to despise, and the men with the yellow
badges on their garments learnt to
cringe and stoop under their load, and
the dark-eyed women with the blue
stripes to their veils lifted them only to
look upon their children. Undeniably,
by every outward test, the poor pariahs
of the Ghetto were degenerate, and
their sad and sordid lives must have
looked both repellent and unpicturesque

to the passer-by.   But it may be doubted
whether the degeneracy went much
deeper than the costume.   If the passer-
by had passed in to one of these gabled
dwellings, when the degrading gaberdine
and the disfiguring veil were thrown
aside, he would have come upon an
interior of home life which would have
struck him as strangely incongruous with
the surroundings.   Amid all the wretched
physical squalor of the street he would
have found little mental and less spiritual
destitution.   If the law of the land bid
Jews shrink before men, the law of the
Book bid them rejoice before God.
Both laws they obeyed to the letter.
Beating vainly at closed doors, they
learnt to speak to the world with bated
breath and whispered humbleness, but
" His courts" they entered, as it was
commanded them, " with thanksgiving,"
and "joyfully" sang hymns to Him.
And the "courts" came to be compre-

hensive of application, and the "hymns" to include much literature. There was always a vivid domestic side to the religion of the Jews, and the alchemy of home life went far to turn the dross of the Ghetto into gold. Their Sabbath, in the picturesque phrase of their prayer-book, was "a bride," and her welcome, week by week, was of a right bridal sort. White cloths were spread and lamps lit in her honour. The shabbiest dwellings put on something of a festive air, and for "*Shobbus*" the poorest *haus frau* would manage to have ready at least one extra dish and several best and bright-coloured garments for her family. On the seventh day and on holy days the slouching peddler and hawker fathers, with their packs cast off, were priests and teachers too, and every day the Ghetto children, for all their starved and stunted growth, had unlimited diet from the *Judengasse* stores of family affection and free schooling. They were probably, however, at no time very numerous, these Ghetto babies, for up to a quite comparatively recent date (1832) Jewish love affairs were strictly under State control, and only fifteen couples a year were allowed to marry.

Ludwig Börne, or Löb Baruch as he is registered in the Frankfort synagogue (1786), was a result of one of these eagerly-sought privileges, and it is easy to see how he came to write, " Because I was born a slave I understand liberty ; my birth-place was no longer than the *Judengasse*, and beyond its locked gates a foreign country began for me. Now, no town, no district, no province can content me. I can rest only with all Germany for my fatherland." An eloquent expression enough of the repressed patriotism which was, perforce, inarticulate for centuries in the *Judengasse* of Frankfort.

Prison as the street must have seemed

to its tenants, there was at least one occasion when its gates had the charms rather
than the defects appertaining to bolts
and bars.   In 1498, a harassed, ragged
little crowd from Nuremberg fled from
their persecutors to find in our Frankfort
Judengasse a safe city of refuge, and for
a century or more the Imperial coat-of-
arms was gratefully emblazoned on the
Ghetto gates as a sign to the outer
world that the Frankfort Jews, though
imprisoned, were protected.   Yet we
may fairly doubt if the feeling of security
could have been much more than skin-
deep, since in 1711, when nearly the
whole of the street was burnt down, we
find that some of the poor souls were so
afraid of insult and plunder, that many
refused to open their doors to would-
be rescuers, and so, to prevent being
pillaged, perished in the flames.   An
oddly pathetic prose version of the
famous Ingoldsby martyr, who " could

stand dying, but who couldn't stand pinching."

When, in 1808, Napoleon made Frankfort the capital of his new grand duchy, the Ghetto gates were demolished, and many vexatious restrictions were repealed. Such new hopes, however, as the Frankfort Jews may have begun to indulge, fell with Napoleon's downfall in 1815. Civil and political disabilities were revived, and it was not till 1854 that the last of these were erased from the statute-book.

The one house in that sad old street, the stirring sermons in whose stones might be "good in everything," would be No. 148, the little low-browed dwelling with the sign of the Rose and Star —a veritable Rose of Dawn it has proved—which was purchased more than a hundred years ago [in 1780] by Meyer Amschel Rothschild, the founder of the great Rothschild house. Every one knows the fairy-like story of that old house; how Meyer Amschel, intended by his parents to be a rabbi, as many of his ancestors had been before him, chose for himself a different way of helping his fellow-men; how he went into commerce, and made commerce, even in the Ghetto, dignified and honourable, as he would have made chimney-sweeping if he had adopted it; how he became agent to the Landgrave of Hesse-Cassel, how faithfully he discharged his stewardship, and how his money took to itself snowball properties, and changed the tiny *Judengasse* tenement into gorgeous mansions. And the old stones would tell, too, of how faithful were the old merchant prince and the wife of his youth to early associations; how sons and daughters grew up and married, and moved to more aristocratic neighbourhoods, but how Meyer Amschel and his old wife clung to the shabby old home in

the Ghetto, and lived there all their
lives, and till she died, some forty years
ago.[1] The very iron bars of those
windows would speak if they could,
saying never a word of their old bad
uses, but telling only how kind and
wrinkled hands were stretched out
through them day by day, and year
after year, dealing out bread to the
hungry. No. 148 could certainly tell
the prettiest story in all the street, and
preach the most suggestive line in all
the sermons carted away with the stones
of the Frankfort *Judengasse.* And it
would be a story with a sequel. For
when all the other sad old houses were
demolished, the walls and rafters of No.
148 were carefully collected and numbered,
and for a while reverently laid aside.
And now, re-erected, the house stands
close by its old site, serving as the

[1] Gütle Rothschild, née Schnapper, died May 7,
1849. Her eldest son, Amschel Meyer Rothschild,
was born June 12, 1773, died December 6, 1855.

centre or depôt for the dispensing of the Rothschild charities in Frankfort. Fanciful folks might almost be tempted to believe that stones with such experiences would be sufficiently sentient to rejoice at the sentiment which refused to let them perish, and which, regarding them as relics, built them up afresh, and consecrated them to new and noble uses.

HEINRICH HEINE: A PLEA.

"That blackguard Heine."—CARLYLE.
"'Who was Heine?' A wicked man."
CHARLES KINGSLEY.

THERE are some persons, some places, some things, which fall all too easily into ready-made definitions. Labels lie temptingly to hand, and specimens get duly docketed — "rich as a Jew," perhaps, or "happy as a king"—with a promptitude and a precision which is not a trifle provoking to people of a nicely discriminative turn of mind. The amiable optimism which insists on an inseparable union between a Jew and his money, and discerns an alliterative

link between kings and contentment, or
makes now and again a monopoly of
the virtues by labelling them " Christian,"
has, we suspect, a good deal to do with
the manufacture of debateable definitions, and the ready fitting of slop-made
judgments.   Scores of such shallow
platitudes occur to one's memory, some
mischievous, some monotonous, some
simply meaningless, and many of the
most complacent have been tacked on to
the telling of a life story, brimful of
contradictions, and running counter to
most of the conventionalities.   The
story of one who was a Jew, and poor ;
a convert, without the zeal ; a model of
resignation, and yet no Christian ; a
poet, born under sternest conditions of
prose, and with sad claims, by right of
race, to the scorn of scorn and hate of
hate, which we have been told is exclu-
sively a poet's appanage—surely a story
hardly susceptible of being summed up

in an epithet. It is a life which has been told often, in many languages, and in much detail; this small sketch will glance only at such portions of it as seem to suggest the clue to a juster reading and a kindlier conclusion.

It was in the last month of the last year of the eighteenth century, in the little town of Dusseldorf in South Germany, that their eldest son Heinrich, or Harry as he seems to have been called in the family circle, was born unto Samson Heine, dealer in cloth, and Betty his wife. That eighteenth century had been but a dreary one for the Jews of Europe. It set in darkness on Heine's cradle, and on his "mattress grave," some fifty years later, the dawn of nineteenth century civilisation, for them, had scarcely broken. "The heaviest burden that men can lay upon us," wrote Spinoza, "is not that they persecute us with their hatred and scorn, but it is by the planting of hatred and scorn in our souls. That is what does not let us breathe freely or see clearly." This subtlest effect of the poison of persecution seemed to have entered the Jewish system. Warned off from the high-roads of life, and shunned for shambling along its bye-paths, the banned and persecuted race, looking out on the world from their ghettos, had grown to see most things in false perspective. Self loomed large on their blank horizon, and gold shone more golden in the gloom. God the Father, whose service demanded such daily sacrifice, had lost something of that divinest attribute; men, our brothers, could the words have borne any but a " tribal " sound? Still, in those dim, dream-peopled ghettos, where visions of the absent, the distant, and the past must have come to further perplex and confuse the present, one actuality seems to have been grasped among the shadows, one ideal attained amid all the grim realities of that most miserable time. Home life and family affection had a sacredness for the worst of these poor sordid Jews in a sense which, to the best of those sottish little German potentates who so conscientiously despised them, would have been unmeaning. Maidens were honourably wed, and wives honoured and children cherished in those wretched Judenstrassen, where " the houses look as if they could tell sorrowful stories," after a fashion quite unknown at any, save the most exceptional, of the numerous coarse, corrupt, and ludicrously consequential little courts which were, at that period, representative of German culture.

The marriage of Heine's parents had been one of those faithful unions, under superficially unequal conditions for which Jews seem to have a genius. It had

4

been something of the old story, " she
was beautiful, and he fell in love ; " she,
pretty, piquant, cultivated, and the
daughter of a physician of some local
standing ; he, just a respectable member
of a respectable trading family, and
ordinary all round, save for the distinction of one rich relative, a banker
brother at Hamburg.

Betty's attractions, however, were all
dangerous and undesirable possessions
in the eyes of a prudent Jewish parent of
the period, and Dr. von Geldern appears
to have gladly given this charming
daughter of his into the safe ownership
of her somewhat commonplace wooer,
whose chiefest faculty would seem to
have been that of appreciation. It
proved, nevertheless, a sufficiently happy
marriage, and Betty herself, although
possibly rather an acquiescent daughter
than a responsive bride in the prelimin-
aries, developed into a faithful wife and

a most devoted mother, utilizing her
artistic tastes and her bright energy in
the education of her children, and finding
full satisfaction for her warm heart in
their affection. Her eldest born was
always passionately attached to her, and
in the days of his youth, as in the years
that so speedily "drew nigh with no
pleasure in them," unto those latest of the
"evil days" when he lay so unconscion-
ably long a-dying, and wrote long play-
ful letters to her full of tender deceit,
telling of health and wealth and friends,
in place of pain and poverty and disease,
through all that bitter, brilliant life of his
Heinrich Heine's relations with his
mother were altogether beautiful, and go
far to refute the criticism attributed,
with I know not how much of truth, to
Goethe, that "the poet had every
capacity save that for love!" "In real
love, as in perfect music," says Bulwer
Lytton in one of his novels, "there must

be a certain duration of time." Heine's attachment to his mother was just life-long; his first love he never forgot, nor, indeed, wholly forgave, and his devotion to his grisette wife not only preceded marriage, but survived it. Poor Heine! was it his genius or his race, or something of both, which conferred on him that fatal *pierre de touche* as regards reputation, "*il déplait invariablement à tous les imbeciles*"?

In the very early boyhood of Heine some light had broken in on the thick darkness, social and political, which enveloped Jewish fortunes. It was only a fitful gleam from the meteor-like course of the first Napoleon, but during those few years when, as Heine puts it, "all boundaries were dislocated," the Duchy of Berg, and its capital Düssel-dorf, in common with more important states, were created French, and the Code Napoléon took the place for a while of that other, unwritten, code in which Jews were pariahs, to be condemned without evidence, and sentenced without appeal. Although the French occupation of Berg lasted unluckily but a few years (1806 till 1813), it did wonders in the way of individual civilization, and Joachim Murat, during his governorship, seems really to have succeeded in introducing something of the " sweet pineapple odour of politeness," which Heine later notes as a characteristic of French manners, into the boorish, beerish little German principality. Although the time was all too short, and the conscription too universal for much national improvement to become evident, German burghers as well as German Jews had cause to rejoice in the change of rule. We hear of no " noble" privileges, no licensed immunities nor immoralities during the term of the French occupation, and

some healthier amusements than Jew-
baiting were provided for the populace.
With the departure of the French troops
the clouds, which needed the storm of
the '48 revolution to be effectually
dispersed, gathered again. Still the
foreign government, short as it was, had
lasted long enough to make an impression for life on Heinrich Heine, and its
most immediate effect was in the school
influences it brought to bear upon him.
Throughout all the States brought under
French control, public education, by the
Imperial edict of 1808, was settled on
one broad system, and put under the
general direction of the French Minister
of Instruction. In accordance with this
decree some suitable building in each
selected district had to be utilized for
class-rooms, the students had to be put
into uniform, the teachers to be French-
men, and all subjects had to be taught
through the medium of that language.

The lycée at Dusseldorf was set up in an ancient Franciscan convent, and hither, at the age of ten, was Heine daily despatched. A bright little auburn-haired lad, full of fun and mischief, and mother-taught up to this date save for some small amount of Hebrew drilling which he seems to have received at the hands of a neighbouring Jewish instructor of youth, Harry had everything to learn, and discipline and the Latin declensions were among the first and greatest of his difficulties. Poet nature and boy nature were both strong in him, and it was so hard to sit droning out long dull lists of words, which he was quite sure the originators of them had never had to do, for "if the Romans had had first to learn Latin," he ruminated, "they never would have had time to conquer the world"—so impossible he found it to keep his eyes on the page, whilst the very motes were dancing in the sunshine as it poured in through the old convent window, which was set just too high in the wall for a safe jump into freedom. One day the need of sympathy, and possibly some unconscious association from the dim old cloister, proved momentarily too strong for the impressionable little lad's Jewish instincts; he came across a crucifix in some forgotten niche of the transformed convent; he looked up, he tells us, at the roughly-carved figure, and dropping on his knees, prayed an earnest heterodox prayer, "Oh, Thou poor once persecuted God, do help me, if possible, to keep the irregular verbs in my head!"

"Jewish instincts," we said, and they could have been scarcely more, for neither at home, at school, nor in the streets was the atmosphere the boy breathed favourable to the development of religious principles. The Judaism of that age was, superficially, very much

what the age had made of it; and its
followers and its persecutors alike combined to render it mightily unattractive
to susceptible natures. Samson Heine,
stolid and respectable, we may imagine
doing his religious, as he did all his
other duties and avocations, in solemn
routine fashion, laying heavy honest
hands on each prose detail, and letting
every bit of poetic meaning slip through
his fat fingers, whilst his bright eager
wife, with her large ideas and her small
vanities, ruled her household, and read
her Rousseau, and, feeling the outer
world shut from her by religion, and the
higher world barred from her by ritual,
found the whole thing cramping and
unsatisfying to the last degree. " Happy
is he whom his mother teacheth " runs
an old Talmudic proverb, but among the
mother-taught lessons of his childhood,
the best was missing to Heinrich Heine
—the real difference between " holy and

4 *

profane" he never rightly learnt, and thus it came to pass that Jewish instincts —an ineradicable and an inalienable, but alas! an incomplete inheritance of the sons of Israel—were all that Judaism gave to this poet of Jewish race.

One lingers over these early influences, the right understanding of which goes far to supply the key to some of the later puzzles. Oddly enough, the clouds which by and by hid the blue are discernible from the very first, and these early years give the silver lining to those gathering clouds. In view of the dark days coming one at least rejoices that Heine's childhood was a happy one; at home the merry, mischievous boy was quite a hero to his two younger brothers, and a hero and a companion both to his only sister, the Löttchen who was the occasion of his earliest recorded composition. It is a favourite recollection of this lady, who is living still, [1] how she, a

[1] Written in 1882.

blushing little maid of ten, won a good deal of unmerited praise for a school theme till a trembling confession was extorted from her that the real author was her brother Harry. His mother too was exceedingly proud of her handsome eldest son, whose resemblance in many ways to her was the sweetest flattery. And besides the adoring home circle Harry found a great ally for play hours in an old French ex-drummer, who had marched to victory with Napoleon's legions, and who had plenty of tales to tell the boy of the wonderful invincible Kaiser, whom one day—blest never-to-be-forgotten vision—the boy actually saw ride through Dusseldorf on his famous white steed (1810). Heine never quite lost the glamour cast over him in his youth ; France, Germany, Judea, each in a sense his *patria*, was each, in the time to come, "loved both ways," each in turn mocked at bitterly enough when the mood was on him, but always with France, the "poet of the nations" as our own English poetess calls her, the sympathies of this cosmopolitan poet were keenest — a perhaps not unnatural state of feeling when we reflect how fact and fiction both combined to produce it. The French occupation of the principality had been a veritable deliverance to its inhabitants, Christian and Jewish alike, and what boy, in his own person, led out of bondage, would not have thrilled to such stories as the old drummer had to tell of the real living hero of it all? And the boy in question we must bear in mind was a poet *in posse.*

In school, in spite of the difficulties with the irregular verbs, Harry seems to have held his own, and to have soon attracted the especial attention of the director. The chief selected for the lycée at Dusseldorf had happened to be

a Roman Catholic Abbé of decidedly
Voltairian views on most subjects, and
attracted by the boy and becoming
acquainted with his family, many a talk
did Abbé Schallmayer have with Frau
Heine over the undoubted gifts and the
delightful imperfections of her son. It
may possibly have been altogether
simple interest in his bright young pupil,
or perhaps Frau Heine, pretty still, and
charming always, was herself an attraction to the schoolmaster, but certain it
is, whether a private taste for pretty
women or a genuine pedagogic enthusiasm prompted his frequent calls, our
Abbé was a constant visitor at Samson
Heine's, and Harry and Harry's future
a never-failing theme for conversation.
What was the boy to be? There was
no room for much speculation if he were
to remain a Jew—that path was narrow, if
not straight, and admitted of small range
of choice along its level line of commerce.

Betty, we know, was no staunch Jewess, and had her small personal ambitions to boot, so such opposition as there was to the Abbé's plainly given counsel to make a Catholic of the boy, and give him his chance, came probably from the stolid, steady-going father, to whom custom spoke in echoes resonant enough to deaden the muffled tones of religion. No question however, of sentiment or sacrifice was permitted to complicate, or elevate, the question; no sense of voluntary renunciation was suggested to the boy; no choice between the life and good, and the death and evil, between conscience and compromise, was presented to him. On the broadly comprehensive grounds that Judaism and trade had been good enough for the father, trade and Judaism must be good enough for the son—the matter was decided.

But still before the lad's prospects

could be definitively settled, one important personage remained to be consulted, the banker at Hamburg, whose wealth had gained him somewhat of the position of a family fetish. What Uncle Solomon would say to a scheme had no fictitious value about it; for even were the oracle occasionally dumb, not seldom would its speech be silver and its silence gold. A rich uncle is a very solemn possession in an impecunious family, so Harry and Harry's poetry, and Harry's powers generally, had to be weighed in the Hamburg scales before any standard value could be assigned to either one of them. For three years the balance was held doubtful; the counting-house scales, accurate as they usually were, could hardly adjust themselves to the conditions of an unknown quantity, which "young Heine" on an office stool must certainly have proved to his bewildered relatives. One imagines him in that correct and cramping atmosphere, fretting as he had done in the old convent school days against its weary routine, longing with all the half understood strength of his poet nature for the green hills and the mountain lakes, and feeling absolutely stifled with all the solemn interest shown over sordid matters.   He tells us himself of some of his "calculations" which would wander far afield, and leave the figures on the paper to concern themselves with the far more perplexing units which passed the mirky office windows, as he complains, "at the same hour, with the same mien, making the same motions, like the puppets in a town house clock—reckoning, reckoning always on the basis, twice two are four.   Frightful should it ever suddenly occur to one of these people that twice two are properly five, and that he therefore had miscalculated his whole life and squandered it all away in a ghastly error"! Many a poem too, sorrowful or fantistic, as the mood took him, was scribbled in office hours, and very probably on office paper, thence to find a temporary home in the Hamburg *Watchman.* What could be done with such a lad? By every office standard he must inevitably have been found wanting, and one even feels a sort of sympathy with the prosaic head of the house who had made his money by the exercise of such very different talents, and whose notion of poetry corresponded very nearly with Corporal Bunting's notion of love, that it's by no means "the great thing in life boys and girls want to make it out to be—that one does not eat it, nor drink it, and as for the rest, why it's bother." It always was "bother" to the banker : all through his prosperous life this poet nephew of his, who had the prophetic impertinence to tell the old man once that he owed

him some gratitude for being born his
uncle, and for bearing his name, was an
unsatisfactory riddle. Original genius
of the sort which could create a bank-
book *ex nihilo*, the millionaire could have
appreciated, but originality which ran
into such unproductive channels as
poetry-book making was quite beyond
him, and that he never read the young
man's verses it is needless to say. Even
in his own immediate family and for his
first book poor Harry found no audience,
save his mother ; and to the very end of
his days Solomon Heine for the life of
him could see nothing in his nephew but
a *dumme Junge*, who never "got on,"
and who made a jest of most things,
even of his wealthy and respectable relatives.

It was scarcely the old man's fault ;
one can only see to the limits of one's
vision, and a poet's soul was not well
within Samson Heine's range. According

to his lights he was not ungenerous. That Harry had not the making of a clerk in him, those three probationary years had proved to demonstration, and in the determination at which the banker presently arrived, of giving those indefinite talents which he only understood enough to doubt, a chance of development by paying for a three years' university course at Bonn, he seems to have come fully up to any reasonable ideal of a rich uncle. It is just possible that a secondary motive influenced his generosity, for Harry, besides scribbling, had found a relief from office work by falling in love with one of the banker's daughters who would seem not to have shared the family distaste for poetry. The little idyl was of course out of the question in so realistic a circle, and the young lady, to do her justice, seems herself to have been speedily reconverted to the proper principles in which she had been trained. No unfit pendant to the "Amy, shallow-hearted" with whom a more recent generation is more familiar, this Cousin Amy of poor Heine's married and "kept her carriage" with all due despatch, whilst he, at college, was essaying to mend his "heart broken in two" with all the styptics which are as old and, alas, as hurtful as such fractures. Poetical exaggeration notwithstanding— and besides her own especial love-elegy, Amalie Heine, under thin disguises, is the heroine of very many of the love poems—there is little room for doubt, that if not so seriously injured as he thought, Heine's heart did nevertheless receive a wound, which ached for many and many a long day, from this girl's weak or wilful inconstancy. Heartache is, however, nearly as much a matter-of-course episode in most young people's lives as measles, and the consequences of either malady are only very exceptionally serious.

Heine's youthful disappointment is of chief interest as having indirectly led to what was really the determining event of his life. When Amalie's parents shrewdly determined on separation as the best course to be pursued with the cousins, and the university plan had been accepted by Harry, his future, which was to date from degree taking, came on for discussion. Except in an "other-worldly" sense there was, in truth, but a very limited "future" possible to Jews of talent. The only open profession was that of medicine, and for that, like the son of Moses Mendelssohn, young Heine had a positive distaste. Commerce, that first and final resource of the race, which had had to satisfy Joseph Mendelssohn, like a good many others equally ill-fitted for it, was not possible to Heine, for he had sufficiently shown, not only dislike, but positive incapacity for business routine.

The law suggested itself, as affording an excellent arena for those ready powers of argument and repartee which in the family circle were occasionally embarrassing, and the profession of an advocate, with the vague "opportunities" it included, when pressed upon young Heine, was not unalluring to him.   The immediate future was probably what most occupied his thoughts ; the freedom of a university life, the flowing river in place of those bustling streets, shelves full of books exchanged for those dreary office ledgers, youthful comrades in the stead of solemnly irritated old clerks.   Whether the fact that conversion was a condition of most of the delights, an inevitable preliminary of all the benefits of that visionary future ; whether the grim truth that "a certificate of baptism was a necessary card of admission to European culture," was openly debated and defended, or silently and shamefacedly slurred over in these family councils, does not appear. No record remains to us but the fact that the young student successfully passed his examination in May, 1825; that he was admitted to his degree on July 20, and that between these two dates—to be precise, on the 28th of June—he was baptised as a Protestant with two clergymen for his sponsors. " Lest I be poor and deny thee " was Agur's prayer, and a wise one ; for shivering Poverty, clutching at the drapery of Desire, makes unto herself many a fine, mean, flimsy garment. With no gleam of conviction to cast a flickering halo of enthusiasm over the act and with no shadow of overwhelming circumstance to somewhat veil it, Heine made his deliberate surrender of conscience to expediency. It was full-grown apostasy, neither conscientious conversion, nor childish drifting into another faith. " No man's soul is alone,"

Ruskin tells us in his uncompromising
way, " Laocoon or Tobit, the serpent
has it by the heart or the angel by the
hand." For the rest of his life Heine
was in the grip of the serpent, and that,
it seems to us, was the secret of his
perpetual unrest. Maimed lives are
common enough; blind or deaf, or
minus a leg or an arm, or plus innumer-
able bruises, one yet goes on living, and
with the help of time and philosophy
sorrow of most sorts grows bearable.
Hearts are tough; but the soul is more
sensitive to injuries, is, to many of us,
the veritable, vulnerable *tendo Achillis*
on which our mothers lay their tender,
detaining, unavailing hands. Heine
sold his soul, and that he never received
the price must have perpetually renewed
the memory of the bargain. He, one
of the " body-guards of Jehovah," had
suffered himself to be bribed from his
post. He never lost the sickening

sense of his humiliation ; it may be read between the lines, alike of the most brilliant of his prose, of the most tender of his poems, of the most mocking of his often quoted jests.

> " They have told thee a-many stories,
>   And much complaint have made;
> And yet my heart's true anguish
>   That never have they said.
>
> " They shook their heads protesting,
>   They made a great to-do ;
> They called me a wicked fellow,
>   And thou believedst it true.
>
> " And yet the worst of all things,
>   Of that they were not aware,
> The darkest and the saddest,
>   That in my heart I bear."[1]

And it was a burden he never laid down; it embittered his relationships and jeopardized his friendships, and set him at variance with himself. " I get up in the night and look in the glass

---

[1] The translation is by Miss Amy Levy.

and curse myself," we find him writing
to one of his old Jewish fellow-workers
in the New Jerusalem movement (Moser),
or checking himself in the course of a
violent tirade against converts, in which
Börne had joined, to bitterly exclaim,
"It is ill talking of ropes in the house
of one who has been hanged." Wherever
he treats of Jewish subjects, and the
theme seems always to have had for
him the fascination which is said to
tempt sinners to revisit the scene of
their sins, we seem to read remorse
between the melodious, mocking lines.
Now it is Moses Lump who is laughed
at in half tones of envy for his ignorant
unbarterable belief in the virtue of un-
snuffed candles; now it is Jehudah
Halevi, whose love for the mistress,
the *Herzensdame*, "whose name was
Jerusalem," is sung with a sympathy
and an intensity impossible to one who
had not felt a like passion, and was not

bitterly conscious of having forfeited
the right to avow it. The sense of his
moral mercenary suicide, in truth, rarely
left him. His nature was too conscientious for the strain thus set upon it ;
his "wickedness" and "blackguardism,"
such as they were, were often but passionate efforts to throw his old man of the
sea, his heavy burden of self-reproach,
and his jests sound not unseldom as so
many untranslateable cries. He had bar-
gained away his birthright for the hope
of a mess of pottage, and the evil taste
of the base contract clung to the poor
paralyzed lips when "even kissing had
no effect upon them." And but a thin,
unsatisfying, and terribly intermittent
"mess," too, it proved, and the share in
it which his uncle, and his uncle's heirs,
provided was very bitter in the eating.
The story of his struggles, are they not
written in the chronicles of the immortals ?
and his "monument," is it not standing

yet " in the new stone premises of his
publishers ? " [1]

His biographers—his niece, the Prin-
cessa della Rocca, among the latest—
have made every incident of Heine's
life as familiar as his own books
have made his genius to English
readers, and Mr. Stigand, following Herr
Strodtman, has given us an exhaustive
record of the poet's life at home and in
exile; in the Germany which was so harsh
and in the France which was so tender
with him ; with the respectable German
relatives, who read his books at last and
were none the wiser, and with the un-
lettered French wife, who could not
read a single word of them all, and who
yet understood her poet by virtue of the
love which passeth understanding, and
was in this case entirely independent of

[1] Messrs. Campe and Hoffmann erected their new
offices during the publication (not too well paid) of the
poet's works.

it. This sketch trenches on no such well-filled ground; it presumes to touch only on the fault which gave to life and genius both that odd pathetic twist, and to glance at the suffering, which, if there be any saving power in anguish, might surely be held by the most self-righteous as some atonement for the " black-guardism."

> "Oh ! not little when pain
> Is most quelling, and man
> Easily quelled, and the fine
> Temper of genius so soon
> Thrills at each smart, is the praise
> Not to have yielded to pain." [1]

Seven years on the rack is no small test of the heroic temperament; to lie sick and solitary, stretched on a " mattress grave," the back bent and twisted, the legs paralyzed, the hands powerless, and with the senses of sight and taste

[1] Matthew Arnold, *Heinrich Heine.*

fast failing. At any time within that
seven years Heine might well have
gained the gold medal in capability of
suffering for which, in his whimsical
way, he talked of competing, should
such a prize be offered at the Paris
Exhibition.[1] And the long days, with
"no pleasure in them," were so drearily
many; the silver cord was so slowly
loosed, the golden bowl seemed broken
on the wheel. His very friends grew
tired. "One must love one's friends
with all their failings, but it is a great
failing to be ill," says Madame Sevigné,
and, as the years went by, more and
more deserted grew the sick chamber.
He never complained; his sweet, un-
grudging nature found excuses for de-
sertion and content in loneliness, in
the reflection that he was in truth un-
conscionably long a-dying. "Never have
I seen," says Lady Duff-Gordon, in her

[1] The Exhibition of 1855.

Recollections of Heine, and she herself was no mean exemplar of bravely borne pain, "never have I seen a man bear such horrible pain and misery in so perfectly unaffected a manner. He neither paraded his anguish, nor tried to conceal it, or to put on any stoical airs. He was pleased to see tears in my eyes, and then at once set to work to make me laugh heartily, which pleased him just as much."

"Don't tell my wife," he exclaims one day, when a paroxysm that should have been fatal was not, and the doctor expressed what he meant for a reassuring belief, that it would not hasten the end. "Don't tell my wife"—we seem to hear that sad little jest, so infinitely sadder then a moan, and our own eyes moisten. Perfectly upright geniuses, when suffering from dyspepsia, have not always shown as much consideration for their perfectly proper wives as does this "blackguard" Heine, under torture, for his.   It is conceivable that under exceptional circumstances a man may contrive to be a hero to his valet, but, unless he be truly heroic, he will not be able to keep up the character to his wife.   Heine managed both.   Madame Heine is still living [1] and one may not say much of a love that was truly strong as death, and that the many waters of affliction could not quench.   But the valet test, we may hint, was fulfilled; for the old servant who helped to tend him in that terrible illness lives still with Madame Heine, and cries "for company" when the widow's talk falls, as it falls often, on the days of her youth and her "*pauvre Henri.*"   There are traditional records in plenty of his cheerful courage, his patient unselfishness, his unfailing endurance of well-nigh unendurable pain. "*Dieu me pardonnera, c'est son métier,*"

[1] Written in 1882.

the dying lips part to say, still with that sweet, inseparable smile playing about them. Shall man be more just than God ? Shall we leave to Him for ever the monopoly of His *métier* ?

DANIEL DERONDA AND HIS JEWISH CRITICS.

George Eliot and Judaism. An attempt to appreciate "Daniel Deronda." By Professor DAVID KAUFMANN, of the Jewish Theological Seminary, Buda-Pesth. Translated from the German by J. W. FERRIER. Edinburgh and London ; William Blackwood and Sons.

THE latest echo from the critical chorus which has greeted "Daniel Deronda" comes to us from Germany, in the form of a small book by Dr. Kaufmann, professor in the recently instituted Jewish Theological Seminary at Buda-Pesth. A certain prominence, which its very excellent translation into English confers upon this work, seems to be due less to any special or novel feature in its criticism

than to the larger purpose shadowed
forth in the title, "George Eliot and
Judaism." It is advowedly " an attempt
to appreciate ' Daniel Deronda,' " and is
valuable and interesting to English
society not as a critique on the plot or
the characters of the book—on which
points it strikes us, in more than one
instance, as somewhat weak and one-
sided—but as indicating from a Jewish
stand-point in how far and how truly
modern Judaism is therein represented.
Unappreciative as the great mass of
the reading public have shown themselves to the latest of George Eliot's
novels, the work has excited a considerable amount of curiosity and admiration on the ground of the intimate
knowledge its author has evinced of the
inner lives and of the little-read literature
of the "Great Unknown of humanity."
We think Dr. Kaufmann goes too far
when he says, " The majority of readers

view the world to which they are intro-
duced in ' Daniel Deronda' as one
foreign, strange, and repulsive. . . . It is
not only the Jew of flesh and blood whom
men encounter every day upon the streets
that they hate, but the Jew under whatever shape he may appear, and even the
airy productions of the poet's fancy are
denounced when they venture to take
that people as their subject" (p. 92).
We think this view concedes too much
to prejudice ; but it is undoubtedly a fact
that the first serious attempt by a great
writer to make Jews and Judaism the
central interest of a great work, has pro-
duced a certain sense of discord on the
public ear, and that criticism has for the
most part run in the minor key. Mr.
Swinburne, perhaps, strikes the most distinctly jarring chord, when, in his lately
published " Note on Charlotte Brontë,"
he owns to possessing "no ear for the
melodies of a Jew's harp," and, disclaiming

"a taste for the dissection of dolls," "leaves Daniel Deronda to his natural place over the rag-shop door" (pp. 21, 22). Even an ear so politely and elegantly owned defective might be able, it could be imagined, to catch an echo from the "choir invisible"; and poetic insight, one might almost venture to think, should be able to discern in poetic aspirations, however unfamiliar and even alien to itself, something different from bran. The arrow is too heavily tipped to fly straight to the goal. There are numbers, however, of the like school who, with more excuse than Mr. Algernon Swinburne, fail to "see anything" in "Daniel Deronda," and a criticism we once overheard in the Louvre occurs to us as pertinent to this point. The picture was Correggio's "Marriage of St. Katharine," and to an Englishman standing near us it evidently did not fulfil preconceived conceptions of a marriage ceremony.

He looked at it long, and at last turned disappointed away, audibly muttering, " Well, I can't see anything in it." That was evident, but the failure was not in the picture. Preconceived conceptions count for much, whether the artist be a Correggio or a George Eliot, and ignorance and prejudice are ill-fitting spectacles wherewith to assist vision.

If it be an axiom that a man should be judged by his peers, we should think that George Eliot would herself prefer that her work should be weighed in the balance by those qualified to hold the scales, and should by them, if at all, be pronounced "wanting." A book of which Judaism is the acknowledged theme should appeal to Jews for judgment, and thus the question becomes an interesting one to the outer world,—What do the Jews themselves think of " Daniel Deronda"? Are the aspirations of Mordecai regarded by them as the expression of a poet's dream, or a nation's hope ? What, in short, is the aspect of modern Judaism to the book ?

"Modern" Judaism is itself, perhaps, a convenient rather than a correct figure of speech. There are modern manners to which modern Jews necessarily conform, and which have a tendency to tone down the outward and special characteristics of Judaism, as of everthing else, to a general socially-undistinguishable level. But men are not necessarily dumb because they do not speak much or loudly of such very personal matters as their religious hopes and beliefs, more especially, if in these days, they are so little in the fashion as to hold strong convictions on such subjects. Our author distinctly formulates the opinion that "men may give all due allegiance to a foreign State without ceasing to belong to their own people" (p. 21); and in the same sense as we may conceive a man

honestly fulfilling all dues as good husband and good father to his living and
lawful wife and children, and yet holding
tenderly in the unguessed-at depths of
memory some long-ago-lost love, so is it
conceivable of many an unromantic-
looking nineteenth century Jew, who
soberly performs all good citizen duties,
that the unspoken name of Jerusalem is
still enshrined in like unguessed-at
depths, as the "perfection of beauty,"
"the joy of the whole earth." Conventionalities conduce to silence on such
topics, and therefore it is to published
rather than to spoken Jewish criticisms
we must turn in our inquiry, and the
little book under review certainly helps
us to a definite answer.

And we may notice, as a significant
fact, that while on the part of general
critics there has been some differing even
in their adverse judgments, and a more
than partial failure to grasp the idea of

the book, there seems both here and abroad a grateful consensus of Jewish opinion that not only has George Eliot truly depicted the externals of Jewish *life*, which was a comparatively easy task, but has also correctly represented Jewish thought and the ideas underlying Judaism. Our author emphatically says, "'Daniel Deronda' is a Jewish book, not only in the sense that it treats of Jews, but also in the sense that it is pre-eminently fitted for being understood and appreciated by Jews" (p. 90) ; and again, "it will always be gratefully declared," he concludes, "*that George Eliot has deserved right well of Judaism*" (p. 95). Does this, then, mean that the " national" idea is a rooted, practical hope? Do English Jews, undistinguishable in the mass from other Englishmen, really and truly hold the desire, like Mordecai, of "founding a new Jewish polity, grand, simple, just, like the old"? (Daniel

Deronda, Book IV.) Do they indeed design to devote their " wealth to redeem the soil from debauched and paupered conquerors," to cleanse their fair land from " the hideous obloquy of Christian strife, which the Turk gazes at as at the fighting of wild beasts to which he has lent an arena " (*ibidem*) ? Was Daniel's honeymoon-mission to the East to have this practical result ? The general Jewish verdict, as we read it, scarcely concedes so much ; it sees rather in the closing scene of Daniel Deronda the only weak spot in the book. Vague and visionary as are all honeymoon antici- pations, those of Daniel, their beauty and unselfishness notwithstanding, strike Jewish readers as even more unsubstan- tial, even less likely of realization, than such imaginings in general. Possibly, as in the old days of the Babylonian exile, " there be some that dream " of an actual restoration, of a Palestine which should be the Switzerland of Asia Minor, which, crowned with ancient laurels, might sit enthroned in peace and plenty,—

"Dispensing harvest, sowing the To-Be."

But save with such few and faithful dreamers, memory scarcely blossoms into hope, and hope most certainly has not yet ripened into strong desire. It may come ; but at present we apprehend the majority of Jews see the "future of Judaism" not in the form of a centralized and localized nationality, but rather in the destiny foreshadowed by our author, in which "Israel will be greatest when she labours under every zone," when "her children shall have spread themselves abroad, bearing the ineradicable seeds of eternal truth" (pp. 86, 87). This conception of "nationality" would point rather to a spiritual than to a temporal sovereignty, to a supremacy of mind rather than of matter, and appears to be in accord with the tone pervading both ancient and modern Jewish literature, which exhibits Judaism as a perpetual living force, maintained from within rather than from without, and destined continually to influence religious thought, and to survive all dispensations.

In his undefined mission to the East Deronda is, therefore, to that extent perhaps, out of harmony with the general tone of modern Jewish thought. We at least are constrained to think that more Jews of the present day would be ready to follow Mordecai in imagination than Deronda in person to Judæa. It is, nevertheless, in strict artistic unity that, shut out for five-and-twenty years from actual practical knowledge of his people, Deronda should represent the *ideal* rather than the *idea* of Judaism. Mordecai, sketched as he is supposed to be from the life, with his deep poetic yearnings, which are stayed on the threshold of action, strikes us as a truer and more typical figure than Deronda hastening to their fulfilment. And on the subject of these same vague yearnings another point suggests itself. We have heard it said that the religious belief of Mordecai centres rather in the destiny of his race than in the Being who has appointed that destiny, and we have heard it questioned whether the theism of Mordecai is sufficiently defined to be fairly representative of Jewish thought, or if Judaism indeed is also passing under that wave of Pantheism which, like the waters of old, is threatening to submerge all ancient landmarks, and to leave visible only "the tops of the mountains" of revealed religion. This seems a criticism based rather on negative than on positive evidence, and derived possibly from the obvious leanings of George Eliot's other writings, and it is, perhaps, somewhat unfair to assume that, even if, on this

point, she does not sympathize with the
Jews, she has any intention of colouring
her picture of modern Judaism with intellectual prepossessions of her own. In
the silence of Mordecai with respect to
his beliefs, he represents the great body
of Jews, whose religion finds expression
rather in action than in formula, and
who are slow to indulge in theological
speculations. Mordecai was true to
Jewish characteristics in the fact that his
belief was concealed beneath his hopes
and aspirations, but had he in any degree
shared the views of the new school of
sceptics, he could not have been the
typical Jew, who sees in the unity of his
people a symbol of the unity of his God.

The pure theism of Judaism may be
said to have its poles in the anthropomor-
phic utterances of some of the Rabbinical
writers, and in the present pantheism of
the extreme German school; but we
should say that the ordinary, the repre-

sentative Jewish thought of the day lies between these two extremes, and, in so far as
it gives expression to any belief on the subject, distinctly recognizes a personal God
presiding over human destiny and natural
laws.　There may be here and there an
inquiring spirit that wanders so far afield
that his attraction towards his people is
lost, and with it the influence his genius
should exert ; but Jewish thought, if own-
ing a somewhat nebulous conception of
the Deity, slowly progressing towards
one fuller and grander, cannot be said to
be drifting towards Pantheism.　Judaism,
unlike many other faiths, has not a history and a religious belief apart,—the one
not only includes and supplements, but
is actually non-existent, " unthinkable,"
without the other.　Thus to have made
an earnest Jew, with the strong racial
instinct of Mordecai, a weak theist, would
have been an inartistic conception, and
Jewish criticism has not discovered this

flaw in George Eliot's exceptional but faithful Jewish portraiture. Judging then, from such sources as are open to us, we are led to infer that the feeling of nationality is still deeply rooted in the Jewish race, and that the religious feeling from which it is inseparable perhaps gives it the strength and depth to exist and to continue to exist without the external props of "a local habitation and a name." Dr. Kaufmann, therefore, very well expresses what appears to be the general convicton of his co-religionists, when he suggests that "in the very circumstance of dispersion may lie fulfilment" (p. 87).

MANASSEH BEN ISRAEL.

PRINTER AND PATRIOT.

WHEN the prophet of the Hebrews, some six-and-twenty hundred years ago, thundered forth his stirring " Go through ! go through the gates ! prepare a way, lift up a standard for the people!" it may, without irreverence, be doubted if he foresaw how literally his charge would be fulfilled by one of his own race in the seventeenth century of the Christian era. The story of how it was done may perhaps be worth retelling, since many subjects of lesser moment have found more chroniclers.

It was in 1290 that gates, which in

England had long been ominously creaking on their hinges, were deliberately swung to, and bolted and barred by Church and State on the unhappy Jews, who on that bleak November day stood shivering along the coast. " Thy waves and thy billows have passed over me" must have lost in tender allegory and gained some added force of literalness that wintry afternoon. Scarce any of the descendants of that exodus can have had share in the return. Of such of the refugees as reached the opposite ports few found foothold, and fewer still asylum. The most, and perhaps they were the most fortunate of the fifteen thousand, were quick in gaining foreign graves. Those who made for the nearest neighbouring shores of France, forgetful, or perhaps ignorant, of the recent experiences of their French brethren under Philip Augustus, lived on to earn a like knowledge for them-

selves, and to undergo, a few years later,
another expulsion under Philip the Fair.
Those who went further fared worse, for
over the German States the Imperial
eagle of Rome no longer brooded, now
to protect and now to prey on its
victims; the struggle between the free
cities and the multitudinous petty prince-
lings was working to its climax, and
whether at bitter strife, or whether
pausing for a brief while to recruit their
powers, landgrave and burgher, on one
subject, were always of one mind. To
plunder at need or to persecute at
leisure, Jews were held to be handy and
fair game for either side.

Far northward or far southward that
ragged English mob were hardly fit to
travel. Some remnant, perhaps, made
effort to reach the semi-barbarous
settlements in Russia and Poland, but
few can have been sanguine enough to
set out for distant Spain in hope of a

welcome but rarely accorded to such
very poor relations.   And even in the
Peninsula the security which Jews had
hitherto experienced had by this date
received several severe shocks.   Two
centuries later and the tide of civilization
had rolled definitely and drearily back
on the soil which Jews had largely
helped to cultivate, and left it bare, and
yet a little longer, Portugal, become a
province of Spain, had followed the cruel
fashions of its suzerain.

By the close of the sixteenth century
a settlement of the dispossessed Spanish
and Portuguese Jews had been formed
in Holland, and Amsterdam was growing
into a strange Dutch likeness of a new
Jerusalem, for Holland alone among the
nations at this period gave a welcome to
all citizens in the spirit of Virgil's
famous line, " *Tros Rutulusve fuat,
nullo discrimine habebo.*" And the
refugees, who at this date claimed the

hospitality of the States, were of a sort
to make the Dutch in love with their
own unfashionable virtue of religious
tolerance.   Under Moorish sway, for
centuries, commerce had been but one
of the pursuits open to the Jews and
followed by the Jews of the Peninsula,
and thus it was a crowd, not of financiers
and traders only or chiefly, but of cultivated scholars, physicians, statesmen,
and land-owners, whom Catholic bigotry
had exiled.   The thin disguise of new
Christians was soon thrown off by these
Jews, and they became to real Christians,
to such men as Vossius and Caspar
Barlæus, who welcomed them and
made friends of them, a revelation of
Judaism.

It was after the great *auto-da-fe* of
January, 1605, that Joseph ben Israel,
with a host of other Jews, broken in
health and broken in fortune, left the
land which bigotry and persecution had

made hideous to them, and joined the peaceful and prosperous settlement in Amsterdam. The youngest of ben Israel's transplanted family was the year-old Manasseh, who had been born in Lisbon a few months before their flight. He seems to have been from the first a promising and intelligent lad, and his tutor, one Isaac Uziel, who was a minister of the congregation, and a somewhat famous mathematician and physician to boot, formed a high opinion of the boy's abilities. He did not, however, live to see them verified ; when Manasseh was but eighteen the Rabbi died, and his clever pupil was thought worthy to be appointed to the vacated office. It was an honoured and an honourable, but scarcely a lucrative post, to which Manasseh thus succeeded, and the problem of living soon became further complicated by an early marriage and a young family. Manasseh had to

cast about him for supplementary means
of support, and he presently found it in
the establishment of a printing press.
Whether the type gave impetus to the
pen, or whether the pen had inspired the
idea of the press, is hard to decide ; but
it is, at least, certain that before he was
twenty-five, Manasseh had found congenial work and plenty of it. He
taught and he preached, and both in the
school-room and in the pulpit he was
useful and effective, but it was in his
library that he felt really happy and at
home. Manasseh was a born scholar
and an omnivorous reader, bound to
develop into a prolific, if not a profound
writer. The work which first established
his fame bears traces of this, and is, in
point of fact, less of a composition than
a compilation. The first part of this
book, " The Conciliator," was published
in 1632, after five years' labour had
been expended on it, and it is computed

6 *

to contain quotations from, or references
to, over 200 Hebrew, and 50 Latin and
Greek authors.   Its object was to
harmonise (*conciliador*) conflicting passages in the Pentateuch, and it was
written in Spanish, although it could
have been composed with equal facility
in any one of half-a-dozen other languages, for Manasseh was a most
accomplished linguist.

Although not the first book which
was issued from his press, for a com-
pletely edited prayer-book and a Hebrew
grammar had been published in 1627,
" The Conciliator " was the first work
that attracted the attention of the
learned world to the Amsterdam Rabbi.
Manasseh had the advantage of literary
connections of his own, through his wife,
who was a great-granddaughter of
Abarbanel—that same Isaac Abarbanel,
the scholar and patriot, who in 1490
headed the deputation to Ferdinand and

Isabella, which was so dramatically
cut short by Torquemada.

Like "The Conciliator," all Manasseh's subsequent literary ventures met
with ready appreciation, but with more
appreciation, it would seem, than solid
result, for his means appear to have
been always insufficient for his modest
wants, and in 1640 we find him seriously
contemplating emigration to Brazil on a
trading venture. Two members of his
congregation, which, as a body, does not
seem to have acted liberally towards
him, came forward, however, at this
crisis in his affairs, and conferred a
benefit all round by establishing a
college and appointing Manasseh the
principal, with an adequate salary.
This ready use of some portion of their
wealth has made the brothers Pereira
more distinguished than for its possession. Still, it must not be inferred that
Manasseh had been, up to this date, a

friendless, if a somewhat impecunious
student, only that, as is rather perhaps
the wont of poor prophets in their own
country, his admirers had had to come
from the outer before they reached the
inner circle.   He had certainly achieved
a European celebrity in the Republic of
letters before his friends at Amsterdam
had discovered much more than the fact
that he printed very superior prayer-
books.   He had won over, amongst
others, the prejudiced author of the
" Law of Nations," to own him, a Jew,
for a familiar friend, before some of the
wealthier heads of his own congregation
had claimed a like privilege, and Grotius,
then Swedish ambassador at Paris, was
actually writing to him, and proffering
friendly services, at the very time that
the Amsterdam congregation were calmly
receiving his enforced farewells.   There
was something, perhaps, of irony in the
situation, but Manasseh, like Maimonides,

had no littleness of disposition, no inflam-
mable self-love quick to take fire ; he
loved his people truly enough to understand them and to make allowances, had
even, perhaps, some humorous perception
of the national obtuseness to native talent
when unarrayed in purple and fine linen,
or until duly recognized by the wearers
of such.

Set free, by the liberality of Abraham
and Isaac Pereira, from the pressure of
everyday cares, Manasseh again devoted
himself to his books, and turned out a
succession of treatises. History, Philosophy, Theology, he attacked them all in
turn, and there is, perhaps, something
besides rapidity of execution which suggests an idea of manufacture in most of
these works. A treatise which he published about 1650, and which attracted
very wide notice, significantly illustrated
his rather fatal facility for ready writing.
The treatise was entitled " The Hope of

Israel," and sought to prove no less than that some aborigines in America, whose very existence was doubtful, were lineal descendants of the lost ten tribes. The Hope itself seems to have rested on no more solid foundation than a traveller's tale of savages met with in the wilds, who included something that sounded like the שמע (Shemang [1]) in their vernacular. The story was quickly translated into several languages, but it was almost as quickly disproved, and Manasseh's deductions from it were subsequently rather roughly criticised. Truth to say, the accumulated stores of his mind were ground down and sifted and sown broadcast in somewhat careless and indigestible masses, and their general character gives an uncomfortable impression of machine-work rather than of hand-work. And the proportion of what he wrote was as nothing compared to

[1] Short declaration of belief in Unity (Deut. vi. 4).

what he contemplated writing. Perhaps
those never-written books of his would
have proved the most readable ; he might
have shown us himself, his wise, tolerant,
enthusiastic self, in them. But instead,
we possess, in his shelves on shelves of
published compilations of dead men's
minds, only duly labelled and cata-
logued selections from learned mum-
mies.

The dream of Manasseh was to com-
pose a " Heroic History," a significant
title which shadows forth the worthy
record he would have delighted in com-
piling from Jewish annals. It is as well,
perhaps, that the title is all we have of
the work, for he was too good an idealist
to prove a good historian. He cared
too much and he knew too much, to
write a reliable or a readable history of
his people. To him, as to many of us,
Robert Browning's words might be applied—

" So you saw yourself as you wished you were—
    As you might have been, as you cannot be—
Earth here rebuked by Olympus there,
    And grew content in your poor degree." [1]

He, at any rate, had good reason to grow content in his degree, for he was destined to make an epoch in the " Heroic History," instead of being, as he wished he were, the reciter, and probably the prosy reciter, of several. Certain it is that great scholar, successful preacher, and voluminous writer as was Manasseh ben Israel, it was not till he was fifty years old that he found his real vocation.   He had felt at it for years, his books were more or less blind gropings after it, his friendships with the eminent and highly-placed personages of his time were all unconscious means to a conscious end, and his very character was a factor in his gradually formed purpose.   His whole life had been an

[1] " Old Pictures from Florence."

upholding of the "standard;" publicists
who sneered at the ostentatious rich Jew,
priests who railed at the degraded poor
Jew, were each bound to recognize in
Manasseh ben Israel a Jew of another
type : one poor yet self-respecting sought
after yet unostentatious, conservative yet
cosmopolitan, learned yet undogmatic.
They might question if this Amsterdam
Rabbi were *sui generis*, but they were at
least willing to find out if he were in
essentials what he claimed to be, fairly
representative of the fairly treated members of his race. So the "way was prepared" by the "standard" being raised.
Which, of the many long-closed "gates,"
was to open for the people to pass
through ?

Manasseh looked around on Europe.
He sought a safe and secure resting-place
for the tribe of wandering foot and weary
heart, where, no longer weary and wandering, they might cease to be "tribal,"

He sought a place where " protection " should not be given as a sordid bribe, nor conferred as a fickle favour, but claimed as an inalienable right, and shared in common with all law-abiding citizens. His thoughts turned for a while on Sweden, and there was some correspondence to that end with the young Queen Christina, but this failing, or falling through, his hopes were almost at once definitely directed towards England. It was a wise selection and a happy one, and the course of events, and the time and the temper of the people seemed all upon his side. The faithless Stuart king had but lately expiated his hateful, harmful weakness on the scaffold, and sentiment was far as yet from setting the nimbus of saint and martyr on that handsome, treacherous head. The echoes of John Hampden's brave voice seemed still vibrating in the air, and Englishmen, but freshly reminded of their rights,

were growing keen and eager in the
scenting out of wrongs; quick to discover, and fierce to redress evils which
had long lain rooted and rotting, and un-
heeded. The pompous *insouciance* of
the first Stuart king, the frivolous *insouciance* of the second, were now being
resented in inevitable reaction. The
court no longer led the fashion, the people
had come to the front and were grown
grimly, even grotesquely in earnest. The
very fashion of speaking seems to have
changed with the new need for strong,
terse expression. Men greeted each
other with old-fashioned Bible greet-
ings; they named their children after
those " great ones gone," or with even
quainter effect in some simple selected
Bible phrase; the very tones of the
Prophets seemed to resound in White-
hall, and Englishmen to have become,
in a wide unsensational sense, not men
only of the sword, or of the plough, but

men of the Book, and that Book the Bible. Liberty of conscience, equality before the law for all religious denominations, had been the unconditional demand of that wonderful army of Independents, and although the Catholics were the immediate cause and object of this appeal, yet Manasseh, watching events from the calm standpoint of a keenly interested onlooker, thought he discerned in the listening attitude of the English Parliament, a favourable omen of the attention he desired to claim for his clients, since it was not alone for political, but for religious rights that he meant to plead.

He did not, however, actually come to England till 1655, when the way for personal intercession had been already prepared by correspondence and petition. His "Hope of Israel" had been forwarded to Cromwell so early as 1650; petitions praying for the readmission of

Jews to England with full rights of
worship, of burial, and of commerce
secured to them, had been laid before
the Long and the Rump Parliament,
and Manasseh had now in hand, and
approaching completion, a less elaborate
and more impassioned composition than
usual, entitled, "Vindicæ Judæorum." A
powerful and unexpected advocate of
Jewish claims presently came forward in
the person of Edward Nicholas, the
clerk to the Council. This large-minded
and enlightened gentleman had the
courage to publish an elaborate appeal
for, and defence of, the Jews, "the most
honourable people in the world," as he
styled them, "a people chosen by God
and protected by God." The pamphlet
was headed, "Apology for the Honourable Nation of the Jews and all the Sons
of Israel," and Nicholas' arguments
aroused no small amount of attention
and discussion. It was even whispered

that Cromwell had had a share in the
authorship ; but if this had been so, undoubtedly he who "stood bare, not cased
in euphemistic coat of mail," but who
"grappled like a giant, face to face,
heart to heart, with the naked truth of
things," [1] would have unhesitatingly
avowed it. His was not the sort of
nature to shirk responsibilities nor to
lack the courage of his opinions. There
can be no doubt that, from first to last,
Cromwell was strongly in favour of
Jewish claims being allowed, but just as
little doubt is there that there was never
any tinge or taint of "secret favouring"
about his sayings or his doings on the
subject. The part, and all things considered the very unpopular part, he took
in the subsequent debates, had, of course,
to be accounted for by minds not quick
to understand such simple motive power

[1] "On Heroes," Lect. vi. "The hero as king,"
p. 342.

as justice, generosity, or sympathy, and both now and later the wildest accusations were levelled against the Protector. That he was, unsuspected, himself of Jewish descent, and had designs on the long vacant Messiahship of his interesting kinsfolk, was not the most malignant, though it was perhaps among the most absurd of these tales. "The man is without a soul," writes Carlyle, "that can look into the great soul of a man, radiant with the splendours of very heaven, and see nothing there but the shadow of his own mean darkness." [1] There must have been, if this view be correct, a good many particularly materialistic bodies going about at that epoch in English history when the Protector of England took upon himself the unpopular burden of being also the Protector of the Jews.

There had been some opposition on

[1] "Cromwell," vol. ii. p. 359.

the part of his family to overcome, some
tender timid forbodings, which events
subsequently justified, to dispel, before
Manasseh was free to set out for England, but in the late autumn of 1655 [1]
we find him with two or three companions
safely settled in lodgings in the Strand.
An address to the Protector was per-
sonally presented by Manasseh, whilst
a more detailed declaration to the Commonwealth was simultaneously published.
Very remarkable are both these docu-
ments.   Neither in the personal petition
to Cromwell, nor in the more elaborate
argument addressed to the Parliament,
is there the slightest approach to the *ad
misericordiam* style.   The whole case
for the Jews is stated with dignity, and
pleaded without passion, and throughout
justice rather than favour forms the
staple of the demand.   The " clemency "
and " high-mindedness " of Cromwell are

[1] Some chroniclers fix it so early as 1653.

certainly taken for granted, but equally
is assumed the worthiness of the clients
who appeal to these qualities. Manasseh
makes also a strong point of the " Profit,"
which the Jews are likely to prove to
their hosts, naïvely recognizing the fact
that " Profit is a most powerful motive
which all the world prefers above all
other things;" and "therefore dealing
with that point first." He dwells on the
"ability," and "industry," and "natural
instinct" of the Jews for "merchandiz-
ing," and for "contributing new inven-
tions," which extra aptitude, in a somewhat optimistic spirit, he moralizes, may
have been given to them for their
"protection in their wanderings," since
"wheresoever they go to dwell, there
presently the traficq begins to flourish."

Read in the light of some recent
literature, one or two of Manasseh's
arguments might almost be termed prophetic. Far-sighted, however, and wide-

seeing as was our Amsterdam Rabbi, he could certainly not have foretold that more than two hundred years later his race would be taunted in the same breath for being a " wandering " and " homeless tribe," and for remaining a " settled " and " parasitic " people in their adopted countries ; yet are not such ingenious, and ungenerous, and inconsistent taunts answered by anticipation in the following paragraph ?—

" The love that men ordinarily bear to their own country, and the desire they have to end their lives where they had their beginning, is the cause that most strangers, having gotten riches where they are in a foreign land, are commonly taken in a desire to return to their native soil, and there peaceably to enjoy their estate ; so that as they were a help to the places where they lived and negotiated while they remained

there, so when they depart from thence,
they carry all away and spoile them of
their wealth ; transporting all into their
own native country : but with the Jews,
the case is farre different, for where the
Jews are once kindly receaved, they
make a firm resolution never to depart
from thence, seeing they have no proper
place of their own; and so they are
always with their goods in the cities
where they live, a perpetual benefitt to
all payments." [1]

Manassseh goes on to quote Holy
Writ, to show that to " seek for the
peace," and to " pray for the peace of
the city whither ye are led captive," [2]
was from remote times a loyal duty
enjoined on Jews ; and so he makes
perhaps another point against that

[1] From " Declaration to the Commonwealth of
England."
[2] Jeremiah, ch. xxix. 7.

thorough-going historian of our day,
who would have disposed of the People
and the Book, the Jews and the Old
Testament together, in the course of a
magazine article. To prove that uncompromising loyalty has among Jews
the added force of a religious obligation,
Manasseh mentions the fact that the
ruling dynasty is always prayed for by
upstanding congregations in every Jewish
place of worship, and he makes history
give its evidence to show that this is no
mere lip loyalty, but that the obligation
enjoined has been over and over again
faithfully fulfilled. He quotes numerous
instances in proof of this; beginning
from the time, 900 years B.C., when
the Jerusalem Jews, High Priest at their
head, went forth to defy Alexander, and
to own staunch allegiance to discrowned
Darius, till those recent civil wars in
Spain, when the Jews of Burgos man-
fully held that city against the conqueror,

Henry of Transtamare, in defence of their conquered, but liege lord, Pedro.[1]

Of all the simply silly slanders from which his people had suffered, such, for instance, as the kneading Passover biscuits with the blood of Christian children, Manasseh disposes shortly, with brief and distinct denial; pertinently reminding Englishmen, however, that like absurd accusations crop up in the early history of the Church, when the "very same ancient scandalls was cast of old upon the innocent Christians."

With the more serious, because less absolutely untruthful charge of "usury," Manasseh deals as boldly, urging even no extenuating plea, but frankly admitting the practice to be "infamous." But characteristically, he proceeds to express an opinion, that "inasmuch as no man is bound to give his goods to another, so is he not bound to let it out but for his

[1] In 1369.

own occasions and profit," "only," and this he adds emphatically—

"It must be done with moderation, that the usury be not biting or exorbitant. . . . The sacred Scripture, which allows usury with him that is not of the same religion, forbids absolutely the robbing of all men, whatsoever religion they be of. In our law it is a greater sinne to rob or defraud a stranger, than if I did it to one of my owne profession; a Jew is bound to shew his charity to all men; he hath a precept, not to abhorre an Idumean or an Egyptian; and yet another, that he shall love and protect a stranger that comes to live in his land. If notwithstanding, there be some that do contrary to this, they do it not as Jewes simply but as wicked Jewes."

The Appeal made, as it could scarcely fail to do, a profound impression; an impression which was helped not a little by the presence and character of the pleader. And presently the whole question of the return of the Jews to England was submitted to the nation for its decision.

The clergy were dead against the measure, and, it is said, "raged like fanatics against the Jews as an accursed nation." And then it was that Cromwell, true to his highest convictions, stood up to speak in their defence. On the ground of policy, he temperately urged the desirability of adding thrifty, law-respecting, and enterprizing citizens to the national stock ; and on the higher ground of duty, he passionately pleaded the unpopular cause of religious and social toleration. He deprecated the principle that, the claims of morality being satisfied, any men or any body of men, on the score of race, of origin, or of religion (" tribal mark " had not at that date been suggested), should be excluded from full fellowship with other men. " I have never heard a man speak so splendidly in my life," is the recorded opinion of one of the audience, and it is a matter of intense regret that this famous speech of Cromwell's has not been preserved. Its eloquence, however, failed of effect, so far as its whole and immediate object was concerned. The gates were no more than shaken on their rusting hinges—not quite yet were the people free to " go through."

The decision of the Council of State was deferred, and some authorities even allege that it was presently pronounced against the readmission of the Jews to England. The known and avowed favour of the Protector sufficed, never-theless, to induce the few Jews who had come with, or in the train of, Manasseh to remain, and others gradually, and by degrees, and without any especial notice being taken of them, ventured to follow. The creaking old gates were certainly ajar, and wider and wider they opened, and fainter and fainter, from friction of unrestrained intercourse, grew each dull rust and stain of prejudice till that good day, within living memories, when the barriers were definitely and altogether flung down. And on their ruins a new and healthy human growth sprang quickly up, " taking root downwards, and bearing fruit upwards," spreading wide enough in its vigorous luxuriance to cover up all the old bad past. And by this time it has happily grown impervious to any wanton unfriendly touch which would thrust its kindly shade aside and once again lay those ugly ruins bare.

Manasseh, however, like so many of us, had to be content to sow seed which he was destined never to see ripen. His petitions to the Commonwealth were presented in 1655, his " Vindiciæ Judæo-

7 *

rum" was completed and handed in some time in 1656, and in the early winter of 1657, on his journey homewards, he died. His mission had not fulfilled itself in the complete triumphant way he had hoped, but "life fulfils itself in many ways," and one part at any rate, perhaps the most important part of the Hebrew prophet's charge, had been both poetically and prosaically carried out by this seventeenth-century Dutch Jew. He had "lifted up a standard for his people."

CHARITY IN TALMUDIC TIMES.[1]

SOME ANCIENT SOLVINGS OF A MODERN PROBLEM.

"WHAT have we reaped from all the wisdom sown of ages?" asks Lord Lytton in one of his earlier poems. A large query, even for so questioning an age as this, an age which, discarding catechisms, and rejecting the omniscient Magnall's Questions as a classic for its children, yet seems to be more interrogative than of old, even if a thought less ready in its responses. Possibly, we are all in too great a hurry now-a-days, too eager in search to be patient to find, for certain it is that the world's

---

[1] Reprinted from *National Review.*

already large stock of hows and whys
seems to get bigger every day. We
catch the echoes in poetry and in prose,
in all sorts of tones and from all sorts
of people, and Lord Lytton's question
sounds only like another of the hopeless
Pilate series. His is such a large in-
terrogation too—all the wisdom sown
of all the ages suggests such an enor-
mous crop! And then as to what "we,"
who have neither planted nor watered,
have "reaped" from it! An answer, if
it were attempted, might certainly be
found to hinge on the "we" as well as
on the "wisdom," for whereas untaught
instinct may "reap" honey from a rose,
trained reason in gathering the flower
may only succeed in running a thorn
into the finger. What has been the
general effect of inherited wisdom on
the general world may, however, very
well be left for a possible solution to
prize competitors to puzzle over. But

to a tiny corner of the tremendous subject it is just possible that we may find
some sort of suggestive reply ; and from
seed sown ages since, and garnered as
harvest, by men whose place knows them
no more, we may likely light on some
shadowy aftermath worth, perhaps, our
reaping.

The gospel of duty to one's neighbour,
which, long languishing as a creed,
seems now reviving as a fashion, has
always been, amongst that race which
taught " love thy neighbour as thyself,"
not only of the very essence of religion,
but an ordinary social form of it. It is
" law " in the " family chronicle " of the
race, as Heine calls the Bible; it is
" law " and legend both in those curious
national archives known as Talmud.
Foremost in the ranks of *livres incompris*
stand those portentous volumes, the one
work of the world which has suffered
about equally at the hands of the com-

mentator and the executioner. Many
years ago Emmanuel Deutsch gave to
the uninitiated a glimpse into that won-
drous agglomeration of fantastically followed facts, where long-winded legend,
or close-argued "law," starts some phrase
or word from Holy Writ as quarry, and
pursues it by paths the most devious,
the most digressive imaginable to man.
The work of many generations and of
many "masters" in each generation,
such a book is singularly susceptible
to an open style of reading and a liberal
aptitude of quotation, and it is no marvel
that searchers in its pages, even reason-
ably honest ones, should be able to find
detached individual utterances to fit into
almost any one of their own preconceived dogmas concerning Talmud. On
many subjects, qualifications, contradictions, differences abound, and instances
of illegal law, of pseudo-science, of
doubtful physics, may each, with a little

trouble, be disinterred from the depths of these twelve huge volumes. But the ethics of the Talmud are, as a whole, of a high order, and on one point there is such remarkable and entire agreement, that it is here permissible to speak of what " the Talmud says," meaning thereby a general tone and consensus of opinion, and not the views of this or of that individual master. The subject on which this unusual harmony prevails is the, in these days, much discussed one of charity ; and to discover something concerning so very ancient a mode of dealing with it may not prove uninteresting.

The word which in these venerable folios is made to express the thing is, in itself, significant. In the Hebrew Scriptures, though the injunctions to charitable acts are many, an exact equivalent for our word "charity" can hardly be said to exist. In only eight

instances, and not even then in its
modern sense, does the Septuagint tran-
slate צדקה (*tzedakah*) into its Greek
equivalent, ἐλεημοσύνη, which would become in English "alms," or "charity."
The nearest synonyms for "charity" in
the Hebrew Scriptures are צדקה (*tzedakah*), well translated as "righteousness"
in the Authorized Version, and חסד
(*chesed*), which is adequately rendered
as "mercy, kindness, love." The Talmud, in its exhaustive fashion, seems
to accentuate the essential difference
between these two words. *Tzedakah*
is, to some extent, a class distinction ;
the rights of the poor make occasion for
the righteousness of the rich, and the
duties of *tzedakah* find liberal and
elaborate expression in a strict and
minute system of tithes and almsgiving.[1]
The injunctions of the Pentateuch con-

---

[1] Maimonides, in his well-known digest of Talmudic
laws relating to the poor, uniformly employs *tzedakah*
in the sense of " alms."

cerning the poor are worked out by
the Talmud into the fullest detail of
direction. The Levitical law, "When
ye reap the harvest of your land,
thou shalt not wholly reap the corners of
thy field" (Levit. xiv. 9), gives occasion
of itself to a considerable quantity of
literature. At length it is enacted how,
if brothers divide a field between them,
each has to give a "corner," and how,
if a man sell his field in several lots, each
purchaser of each separate lot has to
leave unreaped his own proportionate
"corner" of the harvesting. And not
only to leave unreaped, but how, in cases
where the "corner" was of a sort hard
for the poor to gather, hanging high,
as dates, or needing light handling, as
grapes, it became the duty of the owner
to undertake the "reaping" thereof, and,
himself, to make the rightful division ;
thus guarding against injury to quickly-
perishable fruits from too eager hands,

or danger of a more serious sort to life
or limbs, where ladders had to be used
by hungry and impatient folks. The
exactest rules, too, are formulated as to
what constitutes a "field" and what a
"corner," as to what produce is liable to
the tax and in what measure. Very
curious it is to read long and gravely-
reasoned arguments as to why mush-
rooms should be held exempt from the
law of the corner, whilst onions must be
subject to it, or the weighty *pros* and
cons over what may be fairly considered
a "fallen grape," or a "sheaf left through
forgetfulness." Yet the principle underlying the whole is too clear for prolixity
to raise a smile, and the evident anxiety
that no smallest loop-hole shall be left
for evading the obligations of property
compels respect.

Little room for doubt on any dis-
puted point of partition do these exhaustive, and, occasionally, it must be

owned, exhausting, masters leave us, yet, when all is said, they are careful to add, "Whatever is doubtful concerning the gifts of the poor belongeth to the poor." The actual money value of this system of alms, the actual weight of ancient ephah or omer, in modern lbs. and ozs. would convey little meaning. Values fluctuate and measures vary, but "a tithe of thy increase," "a corner of thy field," gives a tolerably safe index to the scale on which *tzedakah* was to be practised. Three times a day the poor might glean, and to the question which some lover of system, old style or new, might propound, "Why three times? Why not once, and get it over?" an answer is vouchsafed. "*Because there may be poor who are suckling children, and thus stand in need of food in the early morning; there may be young children who cannot be got ready early in the morning, nor come to the field till it*

*be mid-day; there may be aged folk who
cannot come till the time of evening
prayer."* Still, though plenty of sentiment in this code, there is no trace of
sentimentality; rather a tendency for
each back to bear its own burden,
whether it be in the matter of give or
take. Rights are respected all round,
and significant in this sense is the rule
that if a vineyard be sold by Gentile to
Jew it must give up its "small bunches"
of grapes to the poor; while if the trans-
action be the other way, the Gentile
purchaser is altogether exempt, and if
Jew and Gentile be partners, that part
of the crop belonging to the Jew alone
is taxed. And equally clear is it that
the poor, though cared for and protected,
are not to be petted. At this very three-
times-a-day gleaning, if one should keep
a corner of his "corner" to himself, hid-
ing his harvesting and defrauding his
neighbour, justice is prompt: " *Let him*

be forced to depart," it is written, *" and what he may have received let it be taken out of his hands."* Neither is any preference permitted to poverty of the plausible or of the picturesque sort. *" He who refuseth to one and giveth to another, that man is a defrauder of the poor,"* it is gravely said.

In general charity, there are, it is true, certain rules of precedence to be observed ; kindred, for example, have, in all cases, the first claim, and a child supporting his parents, or even a parent supporting adult children, to the end that these may be " versed in the law, and have good manners," is set high among followers of *tzedakah.* Then, *" The poor who are neighbours are to be regarded before all others ; the poor of one's own family before the poor of one's own city, and the poor of one's own city before the poor of another's city."* And this version of " charity begins at home " is worked out in another place into quite a detailed table, so to speak, of professional precedence in the ranks of recognized recipients. And, curiously enough, first among all the distinctions to be observed comes this : "*If a man and woman solicit relief, the woman shall be first attended to and then the man.*" An explanation, perhaps a justification, of this mild forestalment of women's rights, is given in the further dictum that "Man is accustomed to wander, and that woman is not," and "Her feelings of modesty being more acute," it is fit that she should be "always fed and clothed before the man." And if, in this ancient system, there be a recognized scale of rights for receiving, so, equally, is there a graduated order of merit in giving. Eight in number are these so-called "Degrees in Alms Deeds," the curious list gravely setting forth as "highest," and this, it would seem, rather on the

lines of "considering the poor" than
of mere giving, that *tzedakah* which
"helpeth . . . who is cast down," by
means of gift or loan, or timely procur-
ing of employment, and ranging through
"next" and "next," till it announces, as
eighth and least, the "any one who giveth
after much molestation." High in the
list, too, are placed those "silent givers"
who "let not poor children of upright
parents know from whom they receive
support," and even the man who "giveth
less than his means allow " is lifted one
degree above the lowest if he "give
with a kind countenance."

The mode of relief grew, with circumstances, to change. The time came
when, to "the Hagars and Ishmaels of
mankind," rules for gleaning and for
"fallen grapes " would, perforce, be
meaningless, and new means for the
carrying out of *tzedakah* had to be
devised. In Alms of the Chest, קופה

(*kupah*), and Alms of the Basket, תמחוי
(*tamchui*), another exhaustive system of
relief was formulated.　The *kupah* would
seem to have been a poor-rate, levied on
all "residents in towns of over thirty
days' standing," and "Never," says
Maimonides, "have we seen or heard of
any congregation of Israelites in which
there has not been the Chest for Alms,
though, with regard to the Basket, it is
the custom in some places to have it,
and not in others."　These chests were
placed in the Silent Court of the
Sanctuary, to the end that a class of
givers who went by the name of
Fearers of Sin,[1] might deposit their
alms in silence and be relieved of
responsibility.　The contents of the
Chest were collected weekly and used

---

[1] יראי חטא (*yeree chet*).　These ultra-sensitive
folks seem to have feared that in direct relief they
might be imposed on and so indirectly become
encouragers of wrong-doing, or unnecessarily hurt the
feelings of the poor by too rigid enquiries.

for all ordinary objects of relief, the
overplus being devoted to special cases
and special purposes. It is somewhat
strange to our modern notions to find
that one among such purposes was that of
providing poor folks with the wherewith
to marry. For not only is it commanded
concerning the "brother waxen poor,"
" *If he standeth in need of garments, let
him be clothed ; or if of household things,
let him be supplied with them,*" but " *if
of a wife, let a wife be betrothed unto
him, and in case of a woman, let a husband be betrothed unto her.*" Does this
quaint provision recall Voltaire's taunt
that "Les juifs ont toujours regardé
comme leurs deux grands devoirs des
enfants et de l'argent"? Perhaps, and
yet, Voltaire and even Malthus notwithstanding, it is just possible that the last
word has not been said on this subject,
and that in "improvident" marriages
and large families the new creed of sur-

vival of the fittest may, after all, be best fulfilled.

Philosophers, we know, are not always consistent with themselves, and if there be truth in another saying of Voltaire's —" Voyez les registres affreux de vos greffes crimines, vous y trouvez cent garçons de pendus ou de roués contre un père de famille"—then is there something certainly to be said in favour of the Jewish system. But this by the way, since statistics, it must be owned, are the most sensitive and susceptible of the sciences. This ancient betrothing, moreover, was no empty form, no bare affiancing of two paupers; but a serious and substantial practice of raising a marriage portion for a couple unable to marry without it. By Talmudic code, " marriages were not legitimately complete till a settlement of some sort was made on the wife," who, it may be here parenthetically remarked, was so far in

advance of comparatively modern legislation as to be entitled to have and to
hold in as complete and comprehensive
a sense as her husband.

But whilst Alms of the Chest, though
pretty various in its application,[1] was intended only for the poor of the place in
which it was collected, Alms of the Basket
was, to the extent of its capabilities, for
" the poor of the whole world." It con-
sisted of a daily house-to-house collection
of food of all sorts, and occasionally of
money, which was again, day by day, distributed. This custom of *tamchui*, suited to

---

[1] We read, in mediæval times, of the existence of
wide " extensions " of this system of relief. In a
curious old book, published in the seventeenth century,
by a certain Rabbi Elijah ha Cohen ben Abraham, of
Smyrna, we find a list drawn up of Jewish charities to
which, as he says, " all pious Jews contribute." These
modes of satisfying " the hungry soul " are over
seventy in number, and of the most various kinds.
They include the lending of money and the lending of
books, the payment of dowries and the payment of
burial charges, doctors' fees for the sick, legal fees for
the unjustly accused, ransom for captives, ornaments
for brides, and wet nurses for orphans.

those primitive times, would seem to be
very similar to the practice of " common
Boxes, and common gatherynges in every
City," which prevailed in England in the
sixteenth century, and which received
legal sanction in Act of the 23rd of
Henry VIII.—" Item, that 2 or 3 tymes
in every weke 2 or 3 of every parysh
shal appoynt certaine of ye said pore
people to collecte and gather broken
meates and fragments, and the refuse
drynke of every householder, which shal
be distributed evenly amonge the pore
people as they by theyre discrecyons
shal thynke good." Only the collectors
and distributors of *kupah* and *tamchui*
were not "certaine of ye said pore
people;" but unpaid men of high
character, holding something of the position of magistrates in the community.
The duty of contributing in kind to
tamchui was supplemented among the
richer folks by a habit of entertaining

the poor as guests ; [1] seats at their own tables, and beds in their houses being frequently reserved for wayfarers, at least over Sabbath and festivals.[2]

The curious union of sense and sentiment in the Talmudic code is shown again in the regulations as to who may, and who may not, receive of these gifts of the poor : "*He who has sufficient for two meals,*" so runs the law, "*may not take from tamchui ; he who has sufficient for fourteen may not take from kupah.*" Yet might holders of property, fallen on slack seasons, be saved from selling at a loss and helped to hold on till better times, by being

[1] Spanish Jews often had their coffins made from the wood of the tables at which they had sat with their unfashionable guests.

[2] This custom had survived into quite modern times —to cite only the well-known case of Mendelssohn, who, coming as a penniless student to Berlin, received his Sabbath meals in the house of one co-religionist, and the privilege of an attic chamber under the roof of another.

"meanwhile supported out of the tithes of the poor." And if the house and goods of him in this temporary need were grand, money help might be given to the applicant, and he might keep all his smart personal belongings, yet superfluities, an odd item or two of which are vouchsafed, must be sold, and replaced, if at all, by a simpler sort. Still, with all this excessive care for those who have come down in the world, and despite the dictum that "he who withholdeth alms is 'impious,' and like unto an idolater," there is yet no encouragement to dependence discernible in these precise and prolix rules. "Let thy Sabbath be as an ordinary day, rather than become dependent on thy fellow-men," it is clearly written, and told, too, in detail, how "wise men," the most honoured, by the way, in the community, to avoid "dependence on others," might become, without loss of casté or respectability, "carriers of timber, workers in metal, and makers of charcoal." Neither is there any contempt for wealth or any love of poverty for its own sake to be seen in this people, who were taught to "rejoice before the Lord." In one place it is, in truth, gravely set forth that "he who increaseth the number of his servants" increaseth the amount of sin in the world, but this somewhat ascetic-sounding statement is clearly susceptible of a good deal of common sense interpretation, and when another Master tells us that "charity is the salt which keeps wealth from corruption," a thought, perhaps, for the due preservation of the wealth may be read between the lines.

On the whole, it looks as if these old-world Rabbis set to work at laying down the law in much the spirit of Robert Browning's Rabbi—

> "Let us not alway say,
> Spite of this flesh to-day,
> I strove, made head, gained ground upon the whole.

As the bird wings and sings
Let us cry " All good things
Are ours, nor soul helps flesh more now than flesh
helps soul."

After this manner, at any rate, are set
forth, and in this sense are interpeted in
the Talmud, the Biblical injunctions to
tzedakah, to that charity of alms-deeds
which, as society is constituted, must, as
we said, be considered somewhat of a
class distinction.

But for the charity which should be
obligatory all round, and as easy of fulfilment by the poor as by the rich, the
Talmud chooses the other synonym חסד
(*chesed*), and coining from it the word
Gemiluth-chesed, which may be rendered
"the doing of kindness," it works out a
supplementary and social system of
charity — a system founded not on
" rights," but on sympathy—dealing not
in doles, but in deeds of friendship and
of fellowship, and demanding a giving of
oneself rather than of one's stores.   And

greater than *tzedakah* write the Rabbis, is *Gemiluth-chesed*, justifying their dictum, as is their wont, by a reference to Holy Writ. " Sow to yourselves in righteousness (*tzedakah*)," says the prophet Hosea (Hos. x. 12); "reap in mercy (*chesed*);" and, inasmuch as reaping is better than sowing, mercy must be better than righteousness. To " visit the sick," to promote peace in families apt to fall out, to " relieve all persons, Jews or non-Jews, in affliction" (a comprehensive phrase) to "bury the dead," to " accompany the bride," are among those " kindnesses " which take rank as religious duties, and one or two specimens may indicate the amount of careful detail which make these injunctions practical, and the fine motive which goes far towards spiritualizing them.

Of the visiting of the sick, the Talmud speaks with a sort of awe. God's spirit, it says, dwells in the chamber of

8 *

suffering and death, and tendance therein
is worship.   Nursing was to be voluntary, and no charge to be made for
drugs ; and so deeply did the habit of
helping the helpless in this true mission-
ary spirit obtain among the Jews, that to
this day, and more especially in pro-
vincial places, the last offices for the
dead are rarely performed by hired
hands.   The "accompanying of the
bride" is *Gemiluth-chesed* in another form.
To rejoice with one's neighbour's joys is
no less a duty in this un-Rochefoucauld-
like code than to grieve with his grief.
A bride is to be greeted with songs and
flowers, and pleasant speeches, and, if
poor, to be provided with pretty ornaments and substantial gifts, but the
pleasant speeches are in all cases, and
before all things, obligatory.   In the dis-
cursive detail, which is so strong a feature
of these Talmudic rulings, it is asked :
" But if the bride be old, or awkward,

or positively plain, is she to be greeted in the usual formula as 'fair bride— graceful bride?'" "Yes," is the answer, for one is not bound to insist on uncomfortable facts, nor to be obtrusively truthful; to be agreeable is one of the minor virtues. Were there anything in the doctrine of metempsychosis, one would be almost tempted to believe that this ancient, un-named, Rabbi was speaking over again in the person of one of our modern minor poets :

> " A truth that's told with bad intent
> Beats all the lies you can invent."[1]

The charity of courtesy is everywhere insisted upon, and so strongly, that, on behalf of those sometimes ragged and unkempt Rabbis it might perhaps be urged that politeness, the *politesse du cœur*, was their Judaism *en papillote*. " Receive every one with pleasant looks,"

[1] William Blake.

says one sage,[1] whose practice was, perhaps, not always quite up to his precepts ; "where there is no reverence there is no wisdom," says another ; and as the distinguishing mark of a "clown," a third instances that man—have we not all met him ?—who rudely breaks in on another's speech, and is more glib than accurate or respectful in his own.

And as postscript to the "law" obtaining on these cheery social forms of "charity" a tombstone may perhaps be permitted to add its curious, crumbling bit of evidence.   In the House of Life, as Jews name their burial-grounds, at Prague, there stood—perhaps stands still —a stone, erected to the memory, and recording the virtues, of a certain rich lady who died in 1628. Her benefactions, many and minute, are set forth at length, and amongst the rest, and before "she clothed the naked," comes the item,

[1] Shimei.

"she ran like a bird to weddings."
Through the mists of those terrible
stories, which make of Prague so miserable a memory to Jews, the record of
this long-ago dead woman gleams like a
rainbow. One seems to see the bright
little figure, a trifle out of breath may
be, the gay plumage perhaps just a
shade ruffled—somehow one does not
fancy her a very prim or tidy personage
—running "like a bird to weddings."
She seems, the dear sympathetic soul, in
an old suggestive sort of way, to illus-
trate the charitable system of her race,
and to show us that, despite all differences
of time and place and circumstances, the
one essential condition to any "charity"
that shall prove effectual remains unchanged; that the solution of the hard
problem, which may be worked out in a
hundred ways, is just sympathy, and is
to be learnt, not in the "speaking from
afar" of rich to poor, but in the "laying

of hands" upon them.   The close
fellowship of this ancient primitive
system is perhaps impossible in our
more complex civilization, but an ap-
proximation to it is an ideal worth
striving after.   More intimate, more
everyday communion between West
and East, more "Valentines" at Hox-
ton, are sorely needed.   Concert-giving,
class-teaching, "visiting," are all helps
of a sort, but there are so many days in
a poor man's week, so many hours in his
dull day.   Sweetness and light, like
other and more prosaic products of
civilization, need, it may be, to be "laid
on" in those miles of monotonous streets,
long breaks in continuity being fatal to
results.

MOSES MENDELSSOHN.

" I WISH, it is true, to shame the oppro-
brious sentiments commonly entertained
of a Jew, but it is by character and not
by controversy that I would do it." [1]   So
wrote the subject of this memoir more
than a hundred years ago, and the sen-
tence may well stand for the motto of
his life ; for much as Moses Mendelssohn
achieved by his ability, much more did
he by his conduct, and great as he was
as a philosopher, far greater was he as a
man.   Starting with every possible dis-
advantage—prejudice, poverty, and deformity—he yet reached the goal of
" honour, fame, and troops of friends "
by simple force of character ; and thus

[1] In the correspondence with Lavater.

he remains for all time an illustration of the happy optimistic theory that, even in this world, success, in the best sense of the word, does come to those, who, also in the best sense of the word, deserve it.

The state of the Jews in Germany at the time of Mendelssohn's birth was deplorable. No longer actively hunted, they had arrived, at the early part of the eighteenth century, at the comparatively desirable position of being passively shunned or contemptuously ignored, and, under these new conditions, they were narrowing fast to the narrow limits set them. The love of religion and of race was as strong as ever, but the love had grown sullen, and of that jealous, exclusive sort to which curse and anathema are akin. What then loomed largest on their narrow horizon was fear ; and under that paralyzing influence, progress or prominence of any kind became a dis-

tinct evil, to be repressed at almost
any personal sacrifice. Safety for themselves and tolerance for their faith, lay,
if anywhere, in the neglect of the outside
world. And so the poor pariahs huddled
in their close quarters, carrying on mean
trades, or hawking petty wares, and
speaking, with bated breath, a dialect of
their own, half Jewish, half German, and
as wholly degenerate from the old grand
Hebrew as were they themselves from
those to whom it had been a living
tongue. Intellectual occupation was
found in the study of the Law ; interest
and entertainment in the endless discussion of its more intricate passages ;
and excitement in the not infrequent excommunication of the weaker or bolder
brethren who ventured to differ from the
orthodox expounders. The culture of
the Christian they hated, with a hate
born half of fear for its possible effects,
half of repulsion at its palpable evidences.

The tree of knowledge seemed to them indeed, in pathetic perversion of the early legend, a veritable tree of evil which should lose a second Eden to the wilful eaters thereof. Their Eden was degenerate, too ; but the "voice heard in the evening" still sounded in their dulled and passionate ears, and, vibrating in the Ghetto instead of the grove, it seemed to bid them shun the forbidden fruit of Gentile growth.

In September, 1729, under a very humble roof, in a very poor little street in Dessau, was born the weakly boy who was destined to work such wonderful changes in that weary state of things. Not much fit to hold the magician's wand seemed those frail baby hands, and less and less likely altogether for the part, as the poor little body grew stunted and deformed through the stress of over-much study and of something less than enough of wholesome diet. There was no lack of affection in the mean little Jewish home, but the parents could only give their children of what they had, and of these scant possessions, mother-love and Talmudical lore were the staple. And so we read of the small five-year-old Moses being wrapped up by his mother in a large old shabby cloak, on early, bleak, winter mornings, and then so carried by the father to the neighbouring "Talmud Torah" school, where he was nourished with dry Hebrew roots by way of breakfast. Often, indeed, was the child fed on an even less satisfying diet, for long passages from Scripture, long lists of precepts, to be learnt by heart, on all sorts of subjects, was the approved method of instruction in these seminaries. An extensive, if somewhat parrot-like, acquaintance at an astonishingly early age with the Law and the Prophets, and the commentators on both, was the ordinary result of this form of education ; and, naturally co-existent with it, was an equally astonishing and extensive ignorance of all more every-day subjects. Contentedly enough, however, the learned, illiterate peddling and hawking fathers left their little lads to this puzzling, sharpening, deadening sort of schooling. Frau Mendel and her husband may possibly have thought out the matter a little more fully, for she seems to have been a wise and prudent, as well as a loving mother, and the father, we find, was quick to discern unusual talent in the sickly little son whom he carried so carefully to the daily lesson. He was himself a teacher, in a humble sort of way, and eked out his small fees by transcribing on parchment from the Pentateuch. Thus, the tone of the little household, if not refined, was at least not altogether sordid ; and when, presently, the little Moses was promoted from the

ordinary school to the higher class taught
by the great scholar, Rabbi Frankel, the
question even presented itself whether it
might not be well, in this especial case,
to abandon the patent, practical advan-
tages pertaining to the favoured pursuit
of peddling, and to let the boy give
himself up to his beloved books, and,
following in his master's footsteps, become perhaps, in his turn, a poorly paid,
much reverenced Rabbi.

It was a serious matter to decide.
There was much to be said in favour
of the higher path ; but the market for
Rabbis, as for hawkers, was somewhat
overstocked, and the returns in the one
instance were far quicker and surer, and
needed no long unearning apprentice-
ship. The balance, on the whole, seemed
scarcely to incline to the more dignified
profession ; but the boy was so terribly
in earnest in his desire to learn, so
desperately averse from the only other

career, that his wishes, by degrees, turned the scale; and it did not take very long to convince the poor patient father that he must toil a little longer and a little later, in order that his son might be free from the hated necessity of hawking, and at liberty to pursue his unremunerative studies.

From the very first, Moses made the most of his opportunities; and at home and at school high hopes began soon to be formed of the diligent, sweet-tempered, frail little lad. Frailer than ever, though, he seemed to grow, and the body appeared literally to dwindle as the mind expanded. Long years after, when the burden of increasing deformity had come, by dint of use and wont and cheerful courage, to be to him a burden lightly borne, he would set strangers at their ease by alluding to it himself, and by playfully declaring his hump to be a legacy from Maimonides.

" Maimonides spoilt my figure," he would
say, " and ruined my digestion; but still,"
he would add more seriously, " I dote on
him, for although those long vigils with
him weakened my body, they, at. the
same time, strengthened my soul : they
stunted my stature, but they developed
my mind." Early at morning and late
at night would the boy be found bending
in happy abstraction over his shabby
treasure, charmed into unconsciousness
of aches or hunger. The book which
had been lent to him was " Maimonides'
Guide to the Perplexed"; and this
work, which grown men find sufficiently
deep study, was patiently puzzled out,
and enthusiastically read and re-read by
the persevering little student who was
barely in his teens. It opened up whole
vistas of new glories, which his long
steady climb up Talmudic stairs had
prepared him to appreciate. Here and
there, in the course of those long,

tedious dissertations in the Talmud
Torah class-room, the boy had caught
glimpses of something underlying, something beyond the quibbles of the schools ;
but this, his first insight into the large
and liberal mind of Maimonides, was a
revelation to him of the powers and of
the possibilities of Judaism.   It revealed
to him too, perchance, some latent possibilities in himself, and suggested other
problems of life which asked solution.
The pale cheeks glowed as he read, and
the vague dreams kindled into conscious
aims : he too would live to become a
Guide to the Perplexed among his people!

Poor little lad! his brave resolves
were soon to be put to a severe test.
In the early part of 1742, Rabbi Frankel
accepted the Chief Rabbinate of Berlin,
and thus a summary stop was put to his
pupil's further study.   There is a pathetic
story told of Moses Mendelssohn standing, with streaming eyes, on a little

hillock on the road by which his beloved
master passed out of Dessau, and of the
kind-hearted Frankel catching up the
forlorn little figure, and soothing it with
hopes of a "some day," when fortune
should be kind, and he should follow
"nach Berlin." The "some day" looked
sadly problematical; that hard question
of bread and butter came to the fore
whenever it was discussed. How was
the boy to live in Berlin? Even if the
mind should be nourished for naught,
who was to feed the body? The hard-
working father and mother had found it
no easy task hitherto to provide for that
extra mouth; and now with Frankel
gone, the occasion for their long self-
denial seemed to them to cease. In the
sad straits of the family, the business of
a hawker began again to show in an
attractive light to the poor parents;
and the peddler's pack was once more
suggested with many a prudent, loving,

half-hearted argument on its behalf. But the boy was by this time clear as to his vocation, so after a brief while of entreaty, the tearful permission was gained, the parting blessing given, and with a very slender wallet slung on his crooked shoulders, Moses Mendelssohn set out for Berlin.

It was a long tramp of over thirty miles, and, towards the close of the fifth day, it was a very footsore tired little lad who presented himself for admission at the Jews' gate of the city. Rabbi Frankel was touched, and puzzled too, when this penniless little student, whom he had inspired with such difficult devotion, at last stood before him ; but quickly he made up his mind that, so far as in him lay, the uphill path should be made smooth to those determined little feet. The pressing question of bed and board was solved. Frankel gave him his Sabbath and festival dinners, and

another kind-hearted Jew, Bamberger
by name, who heard the boy's story,
supplied two everyday meals, and let
him sleep in an attic in his house. For
the remaining four days? Well, he
managed ; a groschen or two was often
earned by little jobs of copying, and a
loaf so purchased, by dint of economy
and imagination, was made into quite a
series of satisfying meals, and, in after
days, it was told how he notched his
loaves into accurate time measurements,
lest appetite should outrun purse. For-
tunately poverty was no new experience
for him ; still, poverty confronted alone,
in a great city, must have seemed something grimmer to the home-bred lad
than that mother-interpreted poverty,
which he had hitherto known. But he
met it full-face, bravely, uncomplainingly,
and, best of all, with unfailing good
humour. And the little alleviations
which friends made in his hard lot were

all received in a spirit of the sincerest, charmingest gratitude. He never took a kindness as " his due ;" never thought, like so many embryo geniuses, that his talents gave him right of toll on his richer brethren. " Because I would drink at the well," he would say in his picturesque fashion, " am I to expect every one to haste and fill my cup from their pitchers? No, I must draw the water for myself, or I must go thirsty. I have no claim save my desire to learn, and what is that to others?" Thus he preserved his self-respect and his independence.

He worked hard, and, first of all, he wisely sought to free himself from all voluntary disabilities ; there were enough and to spare of legally-imposed ones to keep him mindful of his Judaism. He felt strong enough in faith to need no artificial shackles. He would be Jew, and yet German—patriot, but no pariah.

He would eschew vague dreams of
universalism, false ideas of tribalism. If
Palestine had not been, he, its product,
could not be ; but Palestine and its glories
were of the past and of the future ; the
present only was his, and he must shape
his life according to its conditions, which
placed him, in the eighteenth century,
born of Jewish parents, in a German
city. He was German by birth, Jew by
descent and by conviction ; he would
fulfil all the obligations which country,
race, and religion impose. But a
German Jew, who did not speak the
language of his country ? That, surely,
was an anomaly and must be set right.
So he set himself strenuously to learn
German, and to make it his native language. Such secular study was by no
means an altogether safe proceeding.
Ignorance, as we have seen, was " protected " in those days by Jewish ecclesiastical authority. Free trade in litera-

ture was sternly prohibited, and a German grammar, or a Latin or a Greek one, had, in sober truth, to run a strict blockade. One Jewish lad, it is recorded on very tolerable authority, was actually in the year 1746 expelled the city of Berlin for no other offence than that of being caught in the act of studying—one chronicle, indeed, says, carrying—some such proscribed volume. Moses, however, was more fortunate; he saved money enough to buy his books, or made friends enough to borrow them; and, we may conclude, found nooks in which to hide them, and hours in which to read them. He set himself, too, to gain some knowledge of the Classics, and here he found a willing teacher in one Kish, a medical student from Prague. Later on, another helper was gained in a certain Israel Moses, a Polish schoolmaster, afterwards known as Israel Samosc. This man was a

fine mathematician, and a first-rate
Hebrew scholar; but as his attainments
did not include the German language,
he made Euclid known to Moses
through the medium of a Hebrew translation. Moses, in return, imparted to
Samosc his newly - acquired German,
and learnt it, of course, more thoroughly
through teaching it. He must have
possessed the art of making friends who
were able to take on themselves the
office of teachers ; for presently we find
him, in odd half-hours, studying French
and English under a Dr. Aaron Emrich.[1]
He very early began to make translations
of parts of the Scripture into German,
and these attempts indicate that, from
the first, his overpowering desire for self-
culture sprang from no selfishness. He
wanted to open up the closed roads to
place and honour, but not to tread them

[1] Better known to scholars as Dr. Aaron Solomon
Gompertz.

alone, not to leave his burdened brethren
on the bye-paths, whilst he sped on
rejoicing. He knew truly enough that
" the light was sweet," and that "a
pleasant thing it is to behold the sun."
But he heeded too the other part of the
charge, he "remembered the days of
darkness, which were many." He remembered them always, heedfully,
pitifully, patiently ; and to the weary
eyes which would not look up or could
not, he ever strove to adjust the beautiful blessed light which he knew, and
they, poor souls, doubted, was good.
He never thrust it, unshaded, into their
gloom : he never carried it off to illumine
his own path.

Thus, the translations at which Moses
Mendelssohn worked were no transcripts
from learned treatises which might have
found a ready market among the scholars
of the day ; but unpaid and unpaying work
from the liturgy and the Scriptures, done

with the object that his people might by degrees share his knowledge of the vernacular, and become gradually and unconsciously familiar with the language of their country through the only medium in which there was any likelihood of their studying it. With that one set purpose always before him, of drawing his people with him into the light, he presently formed the idea of issuing a serial in Hebrew, which, under the title of " The Moral Preacher," should introduce short essays and transcripts on other than strictly Judaic or religious subjects. One Bock was his coadjutor in this project, and two numbers of the little work were published. The contents do not seem to have been very alarming. To our modern notions of periodical literature, they would probably be a trifle dull ; but their mild philosophy and yet milder science proved more than enough to arouse the orthodox fears of

9 *

the poor souls, who, "bound in affliction and iron," distrusted even the gentle hand which was so eager to loose the fetters. There was a murmur of doubt, of muttered dislike of "strange customs;" perhaps here and there, too, a threat concerning the pains and penalties which attached to the introduction of such. At any rate, but two numbers of the poor little reforming periodical appeared; and Moses, not angry at his failure, not more than momentarily discouraged by it, accepted the position and wasted no time nor temper in cavilling at it. He had learnt to labour; he could learn to wait. And thus, in hard yet happy work passed away the seven years, from fourteen till twenty-one, which are the seedtime of a man's life. In 1750 when Moses was nearly of age, he came into possession of what really proved an inheritance. A rich silk manufacturer, named Bernhardt, who was a prominent

member of the Berlin synagogue, made
a proposal to the learned young man,
whose perseverance had given reputation
to his scholarship, to become resident
tutor to his children. The offer was
gladly accepted, and it may be considered Mendelssohn's first step on the
road to success. The first step to fame
had been taken when the boy had set
out on his long tramp to Berlin.

Bernhardt was a kind and cultured
man, and in his house Mendelssohn
found both congenial occupation and
welcome leisure. He was teacher by
day, student by night, and author at
odd half-hours. He turned to his books
with the greatest ardour; and we read
of him studying Locke and Plato in the
original, for by this time English and
Greek were both added to his store of
languages. His pupils, meanwhile, were
never neglected, nor in the pursuit of
great ends were trifles ignored. In

more than one biography special emphasis is laid on his beautifully neat handwriting, which, we are told, much excited his employer's admiration. This humble, but very useful, talent may possibly have been inherited, with some other small-sounding virtues, from the poor father in Dessau, to whom many a nice present was now frequently sent. At the end of three or four years of tutorship, Bernhardt's appreciation of the young man took a very practical expression. He offered Moses Mendelssohn the position of book-keeper in his factory, with some especial responsibilities and emoluments attached to the office. It was a splendid opening, although Moses Mendelssohn, the philosopher, eagerly and gratefully accepting such a post somehow jars on one's susceptibilities, and seems almost an instance of the round man pushed into the square hole. It was, however, an assured position ; it gave him leisure, it gave him independence, and in due time wealth, for as the years went on he grew to be a manager, and finally a partner in the house. His tastes had already drawn him into the outer literary circle of Berlin, which at this time had its headquarters in a sort of club, which met to play chess and to discuss politics and philosophy, and which numbered Dr. Gompertz, the promising young scholar Abbt, and Nicolai, the bookseller,[1] among its members. With these and other kindred spirits, Mendelssohn soon found pleasant welcome; his talents and geniality quickly overcoming any social prejudices, which, indeed, seldom flourish in the republic of letters. And, early disadvantages notwithstanding, we may conclude without much positive evidence on the subject, that Mendelssohn possessed that valuable indefinable gift,

[1] Later the noted publisher of that name.

which culture, wealth, and birth united occasionally fail to bestow—the gift of good manners. He was free alike from conceit and dogmatism, the Scylla and Charybdis to most young men of exceptional talent. He had the loyal nature and the noble mind, which we are told on high authority is the necessary root of the rare flower; and he had, too, the sympathetic, unselfish feeling which we are wont to summarise shortly as a good heart, and which is the first essential to good manners.

When Lessing came to Berlin, about 1745, his play of " Die Juden" was already published, and his reputation sufficiently established to make him an honoured guest at these little literary gatherings. Something of affinity in the wide, unconventional, independent natures of the two men; something, it may be, of likeness in unlikeness in their early struggles with fate, speedily

attracted Lessing and Mendelssohn to
each other. The casual acquaintance
soon ripened into an intimate and life-
long friendship, which gave to Mendelssohn, the Jew, wider knowledge and
illimitable hopes of the outer, inhos-
pitable world—which gave to Lessing,
the Christian, new belief in long-denied
virtues; and which, best of all, gave
to humanity those "divine lessons of
Nathan der Weise," as Goethe calls
them—for which character Mendelssohn
sat, all unconsciously, as model, and
scarcely idealized model, to his friend.
It was, most certainly, a rarely happy
friendship for both, and for the world.
Lessing was the godfather of Mendelssohn's first book. The subject was
suggested in the course of conversation
between them, and a few days after
Mendelssohn brought his manuscript to
Lessing. He saw no more of it till his
friend handed him the proofs and a

small sum for the copyright ; and it was in this way that the " Philosophische Gespräche " was anonymously published in 1754. Later, the friends brought out together a little book, entitled " Pope as a Metaphysician," and this was followed up with some philosophical essays (" Briefe über die Empfindungen ") which quickly ran through three editions, and Mendelssohn became known as an author. A year or two later, he gained the prize which the Royal Academy of Berlin offered for the best essay on the problem " Are metaphysics susceptible of mathematical demonstration ; " for which prize Kant was one of the competitors.

Lessing's migration to Leipzig, and his temporary absences from the capital in the capacity of tutor, made breaks, but no diminution, in the friendship with Mendelssohn ; and the " Literatur-Briefe," a journal cast in the form of correspondence on art, science, and literature, to which Nicolai, Abbt, and other writers were occasional contributors, continued its successful publication till the year 1765. A review in this journal of one of the literary efforts of Frederick the Second gave rise to a characteristic ebullition of what an old writer quaintly calls, "the German endemical distemper of Judæophobia." In this essay, Mendelssohn had presumed to question some of the conclusions of the royal author; and although the contents of the " Literatur-Briefe " were generally unsigned, the anonymity was in most cases but a superficial disguise. The paper drew down upon Mendelssohn the denunciation of a too loyal subject of Frederick's, and he was summoned to Sans Souci to answer for it. Frederick appears to have been more sensible than his thin-skinned defender, and the interview passed off amicably enough. Indeed, a short while after, we hear of a petition being prepared to secure to Mendelssohn certain rights and privileges of dwelling unmolested in whichever quarter of the city he might choose—a right which at that time was granted to but few Jews, and at a goodly expenditure of both capital and interest. Mendelssohn, loyal to his brethren, long and stoutly refused to have any concession granted on the score of his talents which he might not claim on the score of his manhood in common with the meanest and most ignorant of his co-religionists. And there is some little doubt whether the partial exemptions which Mendelssohn subsequently obtained, were due to the petition, which suffered many delays and vicissitudes in the course of presentation, or to the subtle and silent force of public opinion.

Meanwhile Mendelssohn married, and the story of his wooing, as first told by

Berthold Auerbach, makes a pretty variation on the old theme. It was, in this case, no short idyll of "she was beautiful and he fell in love." To begin with, it was all prosaic enough. A certain Abraham Gugenheim, a trader at Hamburg, caused it to be hinted to Mendelssohn that he had a virtuous and blue-eyed but portionless daughter, named Fromet, who had heard of the philosopher's fame, and had read portions of his books; and who, mutual friends considered, would make him a careful and loving helpmate. So Mendelssohn, who was now thirty-two years old, and desirous to "settle," went to the merchant's house and saw the prim German maiden, and talked with her; and was pleased enough with her talk, or perhaps with the silent eloquence of the blue eyes, to go next day to the father and to say he thought Fromet would suit him for a wife. But to his

surprise Gugenheim hesitated, and stiff-
ness and embarrassment seemed to have
taken the place of the yesterday's cordial
greeting ; still, it was no objection on *his*
part, he managed at last to stammer out.
For a minute Mendelssohn was hope-
lessly puzzled, but only for a minute ;
then it flashed upon him, " It is she who
objects ? " he exclaimed, " then it must
be my hump ; " and the poor father of
course could only uncomfortably respond
with apologetic platitudes about the un-
accountability of girls' fancies. The
humour as well as the pathos of the
situation touched Mendelssohn, for he
had no vanity to be piqued, and he
instantly resolved to do his best to win
this Senta-like maiden, who, less fortunate than the Dutch heroine, had had
her pretty dreams of a hero dispelled,
instead of accentuated by actual vision.
Might he see her once again, he asked.
" To say farewell ? Certainly ! " an-

swered the father, glad that his awkward
mission was ending so amicably. So
Mendelssohn went again, and found
Fromet with the blue eyes bent steadily
over her work; perhaps to hide a tear
as much as to prevent a glance, for
Fromet, as the sequel shows, was a
tender-hearted maiden, and although she
did not like to look at her deformed
suitor, she did not want to wound him.
Then Mendelssohn began to talk, beautiful glowing talk, and the spell which
his writings had exercised began again
to work on the girl. From philosophy
to love in its impersonal form is an easy
transition. She grew interested and
self-forgetful. "And do *you* think that
marriages are made in Heaven?" she
eagerly questioned, as some early quaint
superstition on this most attractive of
themes was vividly touched upon by her
visitor. "Surely," he replied, "and
some old beliefs on this head assert that

all such contracts are settled in childhood. Strange to say, a special legend
attaches itself to my fortune in this
matter; and as our talk has led to this
subject perhaps I may venture to tell it
to you. The twin spirit which fate
allotted to me, I am told, was fair, blue-
eyed, and richly endowed with all spiritual charms; but, alas! ill-luck had added
to her physical gifts a hump. A chorus
of lamentation arose from the angels who
minister in these matters. The 'pity of
it' was so evident. The burden of such
a deformity might well outweigh all the
other gifts of her beautiful youth, might
render her morose, self-conscious, unhappy. If the load now had been but
laid on a man! And the angels pon-
dered, wondering, waiting to see if any
would volunteer to take the maiden's
burden from her. And I sprang up,
and prayed that it might be laid upon
my shoulders. And it was settled so,"

There was a minute's pause, and then, so the story goes, the work was passionately thrown down, and the tender blue eyes were streaming, and the rest we may imagine. The simple, loving heart was won, and Fromet became his wife.

They had a modest little house with a pretty garden on the outskirts of Berlin, where a good deal of hospitality went on in a quiet, friendly way. The ornaments of their dwelling were, perhaps, a little disproportionate in size and quantity to the rest of the surroundings; but this was no matter of choice on the part of the newly married couple, since one of the minor vexations imposed on Jews at this date was the obligation laid on every bridegroom to treat himself to a large quantity of china for the good of the manufactory. The tastes or the wants of the purchaser were not consulted; and in this especial

instance twenty life-sized china apes
were allotted to the bridegroom. We
may imagine poor Mendelssohn and his
wife eyeing these apes often, somewhat
as Cinderella looked at her pumpkin
when longing for the fairy's trans-
forming wand. Possibilities of those
big baboons changed into big books may
have tantalized Mendelssohn ; whilst
Fromet's more prosaic mind may have
confined itself to china and yet have
found an unlimited range for wishing.
However, the unchanged and un-
changing apes notwithstanding, Mendelssohn and his wife enjoyed very many
years of quiet and contented happiness,
and by and by came children, four of
them, and then those old ungainly griev-
ances were, it is likely, transformed into
playfellows.

Parenthood, perhaps, is never quite
easy, but it was a very difficult duty, and
a terribly divided one, for a cultivated

man who a century ago desired to bring
up his children as good Jews and good
citizens. Many a time, it stands on
record, when this patient, self-respecting,
unoffending scholar took his children for
a walk, coarse epithets and insulting cries
followed them through the streets. No
resentment was politic, no redress was
possible. " Father, is it *wicked* to be
a Jew ? " his children would ask, as time
after time the crowd hooted at them.
" Father, is it *good* to be a Jew ? " they
grew to ask later on, when in more
serious walks of life they found all gates
but the Jews' gate closed against them.
Mendelssohn must have found such
questions increasingly difficult to answer
or to parry. Their very talents which
enlarged the boundaries must have made
his clever children rebel against the
limitations which were so cruelly imposed. His eldest son Joseph early
developed a strong scientific bias ; how

10

could this be utilized ? The only profession which he, as a Jew, might enter, was that of medicine, and for that he had a decided distaste : perforce he was set to commercial pursuits, and his especial talent had to run to waste, or, at best, to dilettanteism. When this Joseph had sons of his own, can we wonder very much that he cut the knot and saved his children from a like experience, by bringing them up as Christians ?

Mendelssohn himself, all his life through, was unswervingly loyal to his faith. He took every disability accruing from it, as he took his own especial one, as being, so far as he was concerned, inevitable, and thus to be borne as patiently as might be. To him, most certainly, it would never have occurred to slip from under a burden which had been laid upon him to bear. Concerning Fromet's influence on her children records are silent, and we are driven to conjecture that the pretty significance of her name was somewhat meaningless.[1] The story of her wooing suggests susceptibility, perhaps, rather than strength of heart; and it may be that as years went on the "blue eyes" got into a habit of weeping only over sorrows and wrongs which needed a less eloquent and a more helpful mode of treatment.

If Mendelssohn's wife had been able to show her children the home side of Jewish life, its suggestive ceremonialism, its domestic compensations—possibly her sons, almost certainly her daughters, would have learnt the brave, sweet patience that was common to Jewish mothers. But this takes us to the region of "might have been." Gentle, tender-

[1] Fromet was the affectionate diminutive of *Fromm* —pious. Pet names of the sort were common at that time; we often come across a Gütle or a Schönste or the like.

hearted Fromet, it is to be feared, failed in true piety, and, the mother anchor missing, the children drifted from their moorings.

The leisure of the years succeeding his marriage was fully occupied by Mendelssohn in literary pursuits. The whole of the Pentateuch was, by degrees, translated into pure German, and simultaneous editions were published in German and in Hebrew characters. This great gift to his people was followed by a metrical translation of the Psalms ; a work which took him ten years, during which time he always carried about with him a Hebrew Psalter, interleaved with blank pages. In 1783 he published his " Jerusalem," [1] a sort of Church and State survey of the Jewish religion. The first and larger part of it dwells on the distinction between Judaism, as

---

[1] " Jerusalem, oder über religiöse Macht und Judenthum."

a State religion, and Judaism as
the "inheritance" of a dispersed
nationality. He essays to prove the
essential differences between civil and
religious government, and to demon-
strate that penal enactments, which in
the one case were just and defensible,
were, in the changed circumstances of
the other, harmful, and, in point of fact,
unjudicial. The work was, in effect, a
masterly effort on Mendelssohn's part
to exorcise the "cursing spirit" which,
engendered partly by long-suffered persecution, and partly by long association
with the strict discipline of the Catholic
Church, had taken a firm grip on Jewish
ecclesiastical authority, and was con-
stantly expressing itself in bitter
anathema and morose excommunication.
The second part of the book is mainly
concerned with a vindication of the
Jewish character and a plea for toleration. Scholarly and temperate as is

the tone of this work throughout, it yet
evoked a good deal of rough criticism
from the so-called orthodox in both
religious camps—from the well-meaning,
purblind persons of the sort who, Lessing declares, see only one road, and
strenuously deny the possible existence
of any other.

In 1777, Frederic the Second desired
to judge for himself whether Jewish
ecclesiastical authority clashed at any
point with the State or municipal law
of the land. A digest of the Jewish
Code on the general questions, and
more especially on the subject of property and inheritance, was decreed to
be prepared in German, and to Mendelssohn was entrusted the task. He
had the assistance of the Chief Rabbi
of Berlin, and the result of these
labours was published in 1778, under
the title of " Ritual Laws of the Jews."
Another Jewish philosophical work (pub-

lished in 1785) was " Morning Hours." [1]
This was a volume of essays on the
evidences of the existence of the Deity
and of conclusions concerning His
attributes deduced from the contempla-
tion of His works. Originally these
essays had been given in the form of
familiar lectures on natural philosophy
by Mendelssohn to his children and to
one or two of their friends (including
the two Humboldts) in his own house,
every morning. In the same category
of more distinctively Jewish books we
may place a translation of Manasseh
Ben Israel's famous "Vindiciæ Judæorum," which he published, with a very
eloquent preface, so early as 1781, just
at the time when Dohm's generous
work on the condition of the Jews as
citizens of the State had made its
auspicious appearance. Although this

[1] " Morgenstunden, oder Vorlesungen über das
Daseyn Gottes."

is one of Mendelssohn's minor efforts, the preface contains many a beautiful passage. His gratitude to Dohm is so deep and yet so dignified ; his defence of his people is so wide, and his belief in humanity so sincere ; and the whole is withal so short, that it makes most pleasant reading. One small quotation may perhaps be permitted, as pertinent to some recent discussions on Jewish subjects. "It is," says he, "objected by some that the Jews are both too indolent for agriculture and too proud for mechanical trades ; that if the re-strictions were removed they would uniformly select the arts and sciences, as less laborious and more profitable, and soon engross all light, genteel, and learned professions. But those who thus argue conclude from the *present* state of things how they will be in the *future*, which is not a fair mode of reasoning. What should induce a Jew to waste his time in learning to manage the plough, the trowel, the plane, &c., while he knows he can make no practical use of them ? But put them in his hand and suffer him to follow the bent of his inclinations as freely as other subjects of the State, and the result will not long be doubtful. Men of genius and talent will, of course, embrace the learned professions; those of inferior capacity will turn their minds to mechanical pursuits; the rustic will cultivate the land ; each will contribute, according to his station in life, his quota to the aggregate of productive labour."

As he says in some other place of himself, nature never intended him, either physically or morally, for a wrestler ; and this little essay, where there is no strain of argument or scope for deep erudition, is yet no unworthy specimen of the great philosopher's powers. Poetic attempts too, and mostly

10 *

on religious subjects, occasionally varied his counting-house duties and his more serious labours ; but although he truly possessed, if ever man did, what Landor calls " the poetic heart," yet it is in his prose, rather than in his poetry, that we mostly see its evidences. The book which is justly claimed as his greatest, and which first gave him his title to be considered a wide and deep-thinking philosopher, is his " Phædon."[1] The idea of such a work had long been germinating in him, and the death of his dear friend Abbt, with whom he had had many a fruitful discussion on the subject, turned his thoughts more fixedly on the hopes which make sorrows bearable, and the work was published in the year following Abbt's death.

The first part is a very pure and classical German rendering of the original

[1] " Phædon, oder über die Unsterblichkeit der Seele."

Greek form of Plato, and the remainder an eloquent summary of all that religion, reason, and experience urge in support of a belief in immortality. It is cast in the form of conversation between Socrates and his friends—a choice in composition which caused a Jewish critic (M. David Friedländer) to liken Moses Mendelssohn to Moses the lawgiver. "For Moses spake, and *Socrates* was to him as a mouth" (Ex. iv. 15). In less than two years "Phædon" ran through three German editions, and it was speedily translated into English, French, Dutch, Italian, Danish, and Hebrew. Then, at one stride, came fame ; and great scholars, great potentates, and even the heads of his own community, sought his society. But fame was ever of incomparably less value to Mendelssohn than friendship, and any sort of notoriety he honestly hated. Thus, when his celebrity brought upon him a polemical discussion, the publicity which ensued, notwithstanding that the personal honour in which he was held was thereby enhanced, so thoroughly upset his nerves that the result was a severe and protracted illness. It came about in this wise : Lavater, the French pastor, in 1769, had translated Bonnet's " Evidences of Christianity " into German ; he published it with the following dedication to Moses Mendelssohn :—

" DEAR SIR,—I think I cannot give you a stronger proof of my admiration of your excellent writings, and of your still more excellent character, that of an Israelite in whom there is no guile ; nor offer you a better requital for the great gratification which I, some years ago, enjoyed in your interesting society, than by dedicating to you the ablest philosophical enquiry into the evidences of Christianity that I am acquainted with.

"I am fully conscious of your profound judgment, steadfast love of truth, literary independence, enthusiasm for philosophy in general, and esteem for Bonnet's works in particular. The amiable discretion with which, notwithstanding your contrariety to the Christian religion, you delivered your opinion on it, is still fresh in my memory. And so indelible and important is the impression, which your truly philosophical respect for the moral character of its Founder made on me, in one of the happiest moments of my existence, that I venture to beseech you— nay, before the God of Truth, your and my Creator and Father, I beseech and conjure you—to read this work, I will not say with philosophical impartiality, which I am confident will be the case, but for the purpose of publicly refuting it, in case you should find the main arguments, in support of the facts of Christianity, untenable ; or should you

find them conclusive, with the determination of doing what policy, love of truth,
and probity demand—what Socrates
would doubtless have done, had he
read the work, and found it unanswer-
able.

" May God still cause much truth and
virtue to be disseminated by your means,
and make you experience the happiness
my whole heart wishes you.

"JOHANN CASPAR LAVATER.
" ZURICH, 25*th of August*, 1769."

It was a most unpleasant position for
Mendelssohn. Plain speaking was not
so much the fashion then as now, and
defence might more easily be read as
defiance. At that time the position of
the Jews in all the European States was
most precarious, and outspoken utterances might not only alienate the timid
followers whom Mendelssohn hoped to
enlighten, but, probably, offend the

powerful outsiders whom he was beginning to influence. No man has any
possible right to demand of another a
public confession of faith ; the conversation to which Lavater alluded as some
justification for his request had been a
private one, and the reference to it, moreover, was not altogether accurate. And
Mendelssohn hated controversy, and
held a very earnest conviction that no
good cause, certainly no religious one,
is ever much forwarded by it. Should
he be silent, refuse to reply, and let
judgment go by default ? Comfort and
expediency both pleaded in favour of this
course, but truth was mightier and prevailed. Like unto the three who would
not be "careful" of their answer even
under the ordeal of fire, he soon decided
to testify plainly and without undue
thought of consequences. Mendelssohn
was not the sort to serve God with
special reservations as to Rimmon. Defi-

nitely he answered his too zealous questioner in a document which is so entirely full of dignity and of reason that it is difficult to make quotations from it.[1]   " Certain inquiries," he writes, " we finish once for all in our lives." . . . " And I herewith declare in the presence of the God of truth, your and my Creator, by whom you have conjured me in your dedication, that I will adhere to my principles so long as my entire soul does not assume another nature." And then, emphasizing the position that it is by character and not by controversy that *he* would have Jews shame their traducers, he goes fully and boldly into the whole question. He shows with a delicate touch of humour that Judaism, in being no proselytizing faith, has a claim to be let alone.   " I am so

[1] The whole correspondence can be read in " Memoirs of Moses Mendelssohn," by M. Samuels, published in 1827.

fortunate as to count amongst my friends
many a worthy man who is not of my
faith. Never yet has my heart whispered,
Alas! for this good man's soul. He who
believes that no salvation is to be found
out of the pale of his own church, must
often feel such sighs arise in his bosom."
"Suppose there were among my contemporaries a Confucius or a Solon, I
could consistently with my religious principles love and admire the great man,
but I should never hit on the idea of
converting a Confucius or a Solon. What
should I convert him for? As he does
not belong to the congregation of Jacob,
my religious laws were not made for him,
and on doctrines we should soon come to
an understanding. Do I think there is
a chance of his being saved? I certainly
believe that he who leads mankind on to
virtue in this world cannot be damned
in the next." "We believe . . . that
those who regulate their lives according

to the religion of nature and of reason
are called virtuous men of other nations,
and are, equally with our patriarchs, the
children of eternal salvation." "Who-
ever is not born comformable to our laws
has no occasion to live according to
them. We alone consider ourselves
bound to acknowledge their authority,
and this can give no offence to our neighbours." He refuses to criticize Bonnet's
work in detail on the ground that in his
opinion "Jews should be scrupulous in
abstaining from reflections on the pre-
dominant religion ;" but nevertheless,
whilst repeating his "so earnest wish to
have no more to do with religious controversy," the honesty of the man asserts
itself in boldly adding, "I give you
at the same time to understand that
I could, very easily, bring forward something in refutation of M. Bonnet's work."

Mendelssohn's reply brought speedily,
as it could scarcely fail to do, an ample

and sincere apology from Lavater, a
"retracting" of the challenge, an earnest
entreaty to forgive what had been
"importunate and improper" in the
dedicator, and an expression of "sincerest respect" and "tenderest affection" for his correspondent. Mendelssohn's was a nature to have more
sympathy with the errors incidental to
too much than to too little zeal, and the
apology was accepted as generously as it
was offered. And here ended, so far as
the principals were concerned, this somewhat unique specimen of a literary
squabble. A crowd of lesser writers,
unfortunately, hastened to make capital
out of it ; and a bewildering mist of
nondescript and pedantic compositions
soon darkened the literary firmament,
obscuring and vulgarizing the whole
subject. They took "sides" and gave
"views" of the controversy ; but Mendelssohn answered none and read as few

as possible of these publications. Still
the strain and worry told on his sensitive
and peace-loving nature, and he did not
readily recover his old elasticity of
temperament.

In 1778 Lessing's wife died, and his
friend's trouble touched deep chords
both of sympathy and of memory in
Mendelssohn. Yet more cruelly were
they jarred when, two years later, Lessing
himself followed, and an uninterrupted
friendship of over thirty years was thus
dissolved. Lessing and Mendelssohn
had been to each other the sober
realization of the beautiful ideal embodied
in the drama of " Nathan der Weise."
"What to you makes me seem Christian
makes of you the Jew to me," each
could most truly say to the other. They
helped the world to see it too, and to
recognize the Divine truth that " to be to
the best thou knowest ever true is all
the creed."

The death of his friend was a terrible blow to Mendelssohn. "After wrinkles come," says Mr. Lowell, in likening ancient friendships to slow-growing trees, "few plant, but water dead ones with vain tears." In this case, the actual pain of loss was greatly aggravated by some publications which appeared shortly after Lessing's death, impugning his sincerity and religious feeling. Germany, as Goethe once bitterly remarked, "needs time to be thankful." In the first year or two following Lessing's death it was, perhaps, too early to expect gratitude from his country for the lustre his talents had shed on it. Some of the pamphlets would make it seem that it was too early even for decency. Mendelssohn vigorously took up the cudgels for his dead friend ; too vigorously perhaps, since Kant remarked that " it is Mendelssohn's fault, if Jacobi (the most notorious of the assailants) should now consider himself a philosopher." To Mendelssohn's warm-hearted, generous nature it would, however, have been impossible to remain silent when one whom he knew to be tolerant, earnest, and sincere in the fullest sense of those words of highest praise, was accused of "covert Spinozism;" a charge which again was broadly rendered, by these wretched ignorant interpreters of a language they failed to understand, as atheism and hypocrisy.

This was his last literary work. It shows no sign of decaying powers; it is full of pathos, of wit, of clear close reasoning, and of brilliant satire; yet nevertheless it was his monument as well as his friend's. He took the manuscript to his publisher in the last day of the year 1785; and in the first week of the New Year 1786, still only fifty-six years old, he quietly and painlessly died. That last work seems to make a beautiful and fitting end to his life; a life which truly adds a worthy stanza to what Herder calls "the greatest poem of all time—the history of the Jews."